"Most couples genuinely desire an intimate relationship. *Emotional Fitness for Intimacy* is filled with insights and exercises that will enhance the intimacy level in any relationship. For couples who would like to see dreams become reality, Goldsmith points the way."

—Gary D. Chapman, author of *The Five Love Languages* and *Love As a Way of Life*

"This book is an encyclopedia of wise and useful information for couples who want to deepen their relationship. Written by a wise and experienced therapist, couples will find exercises to help them discover and accept differences, deepen connection, and achieve intimacy. I recommend it to all couples."

—Harville Hendrix, Ph.D., author of *Getting the Love You Want*

"In this fascinating book, Goldsmith reveals how to keep intimacy alive in relationships, a beautiful gift to his readers."

—Judith Orloff, MD, author of *Positive Energy*

"I found much wisdom in this book expressed in ways which were practical and easy to understand and incorporate into one's lifestyle."

—Bernie Siegel, MD, author of *Love, Magic, and Mudpies* and *365 Prescriptions for Living*

"If we value intimacy as much as we say we do, and if it were possible to construct a handbook covering the complexity of relationship, Goldsmith's *Emotional Fitness for Intimacy* is it. Organized in manageable chunks, full of practical suggestions, and informed by a sagacity which both illumines and facilitates intimacy, this book brings each reader to more thoughtful, practical possibilities for his or her relationship."

—James Hollis, Ph.D., Jungian analyst and author of *What Matters Most*

"*Emotional Fitness for Intimacy* offers compelling, practical advice for understanding true intimacy and for achieving our goals in a successful love relationship. Goldsmith provides tips for challenging situations and compromising positions we all face in our love lives, and those who read his book will be ahead in the unending quest for a healthy, rewarding emotional connection.

—Susan Shapiro Barash, author of *Little White Lies, Deep Dark Secrets*

Emotional Fitness
for Intimacy

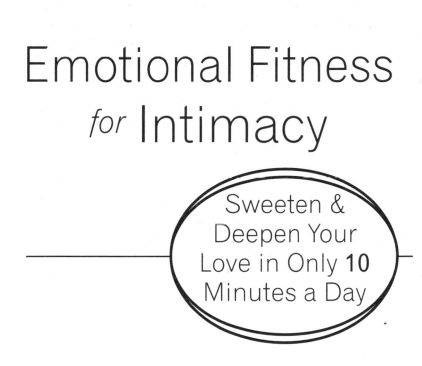

Sweeten &
Deepen Your
Love in Only **10**
Minutes a Day

BARTON GOLDSMITH, PH.D.

New Harbinger Publications, Inc.

Distributed in Canada by Raincoast Books

Copyright © 2009 by Barton Goldsmith
    New Harbinger Publications, Inc.
    5674 Shattuck Avenue
    Oakland, CA 94609
    www.newharbinger.com

Cover and text design by Amy Shoup; Acquired by Melissa Kirk; Edited by Brady Kahn

---

Library of Congress Cataloging-in-Publication Data

Goldsmith, Barton.
 Emotional fitness for intimacy : sweeten and deepen your love in only 10 minutes a day / Barton Goldsmith.
    p. cm.
 Includes bibliographical references.
 ISBN-13: 978-1-57224-647-8 (pbk. : alk. paper)
 ISBN-10: 1-57224-647-2 (pbk. : alk. paper)
 1. Intimacy (Psychology) 2. Communication in marriage. 3. Man-woman relationships. I. Title.
 BF575.I5.G55 2009
 158.2'4--dc22

2008052323

11   10   09

10   9   8   7   6   5   4   3   2   1

First printing

To Keaton and Oliver, bright flowers in the garden of my life.
May your love and intimacy last longer than time.

Contents

Acknowledgments

At New Harbinger Publications, I'd like to thank publisher Matt McKay, acquisitions editor Melissa Kirk, and publicity maven Earlita Chenault. I would also like to thank my copyeditor, Brady Kahn.

This book wouldn't exist if not for the readers and editors of my column, and I will be forever grateful to the Ventura *County Star* and Scripps Howard News Service for their unwavering support, as well as to the editors of the two hundred–plus papers who have graciously run my articles.

The team (and my dear friends) at KCLU/NPR have been nothing but supportive, innovative, and just plain fun to be around. They include Mary Olson, Jim Rondeau, Lance Orozco, Mia Karnatz-Shifflett, and Jocelyne Rohrback. Thank you also to the many guests who have shared their wisdom with our listening audience.

My team at the office, Mary Trudeau and Wendy Cherry, make my life work—and I also get to enjoy their company.

I am honored to have learned from my colleagues, including Stephen Trudeau, Harville Hendrix, Bernie Siegel, Scott James, Michael Agress, William Glasser, Judith Orloff, Gary Chapman, Linda Metzger, Jeffery Zeig, Linda Loomis, James Hollis, Susan Shapiro Barash, Linda Gerrits, and Louise L. Hay. Some of my mentors have passed on; I acknowledge with gratitude the late Albert Ellis, David Viscott, and Elizabeth Kubler-Ross.

To my loving family and lifelong friends Michael Park; Kevin Connelly; Shelley MacEwen; Nancy, David, and Nina Padberg; Brenda and John James; Kevin Hanley; Rebecca Love; David and Dan Richmond; Jeb Adams; Jason Love; Trygve Duryea; Robert Scully; Leigh Leshner; and the dearly departed Indus Arthur: thank you for sharing your time with me.

I am deeply humbled to have received several professional awards and wish to thank the American Association of Marriage and Family Therapists for the Peter Markin Award for Humanitarian Acts, the California Association of Alcoholism and Drug Abuse Counselors for the Joseph Giannantoino Award for the Outstanding Educator of the Year, and the

California Association of Marriage and Family Therapists for the Clark Vincent Award for Writing.

And finally, I thank Silva, who has my heart and teaches me the true meaning of intimacy.

Introduction

$\mathcal{C}$reating greater intimacy is more about internal energy than it is about overt actions. It is about feeling things that you never have felt before. It is about changing your life view and understanding that if you do your relationship right, it is intimate. If you are in a place where you feel totally safe from the world when you are in your lover's arms, that's intimacy. This is not to be confused with that giddy invasion of feeling like you're in uncharted waters as you bask in each other's love.

When a couple is truly intimate, their comfort levels rise. The bond just *is* and it defies analysis. When you're connected in a way that makes other people envious of your love, that's intimacy. We've all seen couples who are obviously in love. And many times, if we are not in the same place in our relationship, we may question the validity of where we are. Yet where you are in your relationship is the best place to start.

In fact it is imperative that you embrace your current level of intimacy in order to move forward.

To get to the next level, you may be thinking that you want to move in with your partner, buy a house, or get married. You may believe that taking these actions will create greater intimacy in your relationship. What they may do is give you the opportunity to get closer and create more depth. But to achieve that, you have to do something else, and that is what this book is all about.

There are fifty-two lessons in this book, so it's kind of like weekly therapy if you want to use it that way. There are also hundreds of tips and dozens of exercises designed to create greater closeness. Some of these concepts you may already be familiar with but perhaps over time have forgotten to use. We all do it. As you read this book together, think of it as a checklist or a gentle reminder to help you strengthen the sweetest and deepest of life's experiences, your intimate relationship.

Remember that intimacy is an emotion, not an activity or an exercise. That being said, I have created these exercises specifically to enhance the depth of intimacy in your relationship. Whether you have been working on your partnership for some time or are in the early months of your romance and are eager to get as close as possible, investing just ten minutes a day will get you to the next level. From there, you can go wherever you choose.

PART
1

Intimate

Relationships

True Love vs. In Love

I have had many people sit on the therapy couch, look deeply at their partner, and say, "I love you, but I'm not in love with you." As the eyes of their other half fill with tears, I explain to both of them that this is not a bad thing. Now they can get down to the business of having a real relationship and loving each other as two people should.

Hey, you know I'm all about intimacy, and being in love is a great rush. The problem is that the hangover from this kind of infatuation can kill you. Many people are not rational when they're in love, and some have a tendency to suffer deep depression if the relationship ends.

Everyone wants to be in love, and why? Because it feels soooo good. Being in love creates activity in the brain that sends little electrical impulses throughout our bodies, making us feel all atwitter. The problem is that for most couples being in love almost never lasts forever. Yes, a few wedded pairs are able to stay connected in that way, but it's not the norm.

The feelings we have while we are in love make us feel immortal, brilliant, powerful, and just plain wonderful. Unfortunately, being in love also creates a kind of emotional blindness.

While we are in love, we don't contemplate if a partner will be willing or able to take care of us when we are sick, if he or she is ready to become a parent, or how we're going to pay for the mortgage on that dream house.

True love is a combination of emotions and actions, including talking, tenderness, and trust. These behaviors are an ample replacement for the heart-pounding, sexual excitement of being in love. Your drive changes from needing to be with the other person to wanting to care for him or her, and you can still have a hot and heavy romantic relationship in the process.

Making the shift from not feeling "in love" to treasuring the feelings of true love may seem a little awkward at first, but with some time and effort, the rewards are priceless. Nothing can take the place of two hearts becoming one for a lifetime.

Here are a couple of tips for easing the transition from being in love to feeling true love.

♡ *If you are married or had a commitment ceremony, suggest to your partner that you invite all your friends over for a party without telling them that you are reaffirming your wedding vows. This surprise ceremony will make everyone feel the love you have for each other. Not only will you feel the love returned from your partner, but having it witnessed by the people who care for you will create a powerful and enduring* memory. Yes, this will take more than ten minutes, but the joy will last forever.

♡ There's truth to the saying that you don't know what you've got until it's gone. This exercise is not for the faint of heart. It's profound and a bit dark: the next time you are away from your love, imagine that you are all alone. She or he isn't there anymore. What would your life look like? Feel the loss, and cry the tears. You'll wake up the next day feeling more inspired than ever to do what it takes to deepen and strengthen your relationship.

From Me to We

$\mathscr{B}$ecoming a "we" when you have spent most of your life being a "me" can take a bit of getting used to. It's true that self-identity plays an important part in basic survival, but focusing too much on "I" after you've said "I'm yours" can be problematic.

A well-respected school of thought teaches that when speaking of relationship issues, it is appropriate to use *I-statements*. For example, instead of saying "You make me feel guilty," you should say, "I feel guilty." This mitigates blame and, therefore, defensiveness and allows a conversation to happen. I'm all for that, but I think there may be a greater need for *we-statements*.

When two people become a couple, on some level everything that happens to one of you also happens to the other. Illness, job change, good news and bad, send ripples through a relationship like a stone thrown in a pond of still water. I don't want to get too Zen about this, but it's reality, and once you recognize it, your relationship can achieve a level of joy and intimacy that most only dream about.

You have to look at your behaviors in a different way once you've bonded with another. For example, if you're in a bad mood and you're alone, you can do whatever you want, be silent, swear at the TV, whatever. When you're in a relationship and you project your feelings onto your partner, your partner will sense that you're going through something and thus change the way he or she is interacting with you. That can mean withdrawing or shutting down if you escalate. Eventually, if you continue to behave as though it doesn't affect your partner, you may not have one, so take this thinking to heart. By the way, a sensitive mate can usually see a mood coming and, with "we" attitude in gear, may be able to circumvent an uncomfortable situation.

To find greater depth in your relationship, you need to move away from independence and avoid codependence to create an interdependence. This is when two people revolve around each other, are able to connect with each other completely whenever the desire arises, and also feel that they have their own lives. This enlightened state of being in a relationship gives both partners the best of each other and of themselves.

Couples who think in terms of "we" versus "me" also experience less stress when it comes to money issues. There is the desire to not overburden your partner and to spend as well as contribute in a balanced manner. Imagine what life would be like if at the end of the month there were no surprises, all the bills were paid, and there was enough left over to save a little and spend a little. Just keep in mind that you're part of a couple and everything you put in or take out of the pot has an effect on how you will live.

Life as a "we" won't fray the fabric of your individuality. In truth, it weaves in a new dimension that allows you to get more out of life by experiencing it through the heart of another.

Here are a couple of tips to help you enjoy being a "we."

♡ *Take ten minutes out of your day to verbalize your feelings for your partner and reaffirm your commitment. Tell your partner how grateful you are to have him or her in your life. This doesn't have to be done every day, but doing it a couple of times a week will make you closer and help you both to feel like you're a "we."*

♡ *If you need to resolve an issue, sit down with your partner and discuss it. Make sure that each of you has an opportunity to talk and to be heard. For example, if your partner has an issue, let him or her talk for several minutes, then take a minute to respond. It's important to paraphrase what your partner has just said so that he or she feels that you understand. Make sure that you fully hear your partner before expressing your own concerns. Then if you want to say something, it's your turn to talk and have your partner respond in similar fashion. Getting the emotions out of your head while you're being gently supported is an intimate experience and will deepen your relationship.*

Make the Effort

One of the things that I see in successful relationships is that both people will go the extra mile to make their partner happy.

Sometimes this means remembering the anniversary of their first date, bringing flowers, cooking something special, or giving a back rub without being asked. This really makes a difference if one of you has had a hard day or if there has been an uncomfortable moment between you.

Any time two adults are together, there are going to be times when you step on each other's toes. What makes the difference between happy couples and those who struggle is that in the positive relationships, the people in them do what they can to make things better sooner rather than later. They also remember to do nice things for no good reason from time to time as a way of showing their love.

You can say "I love you" until you're blue in the face, but unless your actions follow suit, your partner isn't going to get it. In fact the words (which are powerful) will lose their meaning and distance will grow between you. Many people want to hear the words, but we all need to see the actions.

This is especially true when you have had a disagreement. It's very easy to become self-righteous and act out your displeasure. You're a true adult when you can say to yourself, "We've just butted heads and now it's up to me to show that I care by doing the appropriate thing." What that thing is can be as different as the people involved. From making an apology and asking for forgiveness to serenading your partner while she or he is in the shower, you need to do something to change the energy between you.

Making an effort says it all, and it will make your time together better. It's sad to watch people hurt one another by holding on to anger or to hurt that can so easily be transmuted. All it takes is a willingness to react differently. There's too much pain in the world to make room for it in your relationship.

The truth is that you have the power here. Life is too short to stay upset any longer than you have to. So the next time you and your special someone have a disagreement or accidentally rub each other the wrong way, make the effort. E-mail or send a card or some flowers, or show up for your partner in a way that says you care. It isn't that difficult and it doesn't have to cost you anything. In this case, all you ever have to pay is attention.

Here are some tips to help you to make the effort effortless.

♡ *Make the first move to get over a conflict, even if you think it's the other person's fault. If you feel things are out of balance, you can make a difference by starting a conversation or even making a joke. If you're having a difficult moment, you can say, "Hey, let's not stay in this mood. Let's agree to both be over it in ten minutes." Then ask, "Is there anything I can do to assist you in your process?" If you need some extra support, say something like, "Can you please give me ten minutes of your undivided attention, so I can release this negative energy I'm feeling?" Your willingness to engage in the activity will shift the dynamic between you, and you will also heal the hurt.*

♡ *Ask your partner to make a list of things you could do that would make him or her feel adored by you. You make a list for your partner as well. Then make a date night to exchange lists. This exchange will bring you closer. And once you have the list, you and your partner can create intimate moments for each other whenever you want.*

Intimacy Makes Us Vulnerable

*I*ntimacy, by its very nature, requires us to be vulnerable. Our partner, lover, or mate can know us to our very core, sometimes better than we know ourselves, and that can make anyone feel as though they are totally exposed. Intimacy can be intimidating. However, it is also an amazingly freeing experience to be completely who you are with someone you totally trust

Allowing yourself to be open gives you the opportunity to let your loved one's heart touch your own, and the loneliness in life melts away with every tender moment you let in. Despite its benefits, for many people this idea is terribly frightening. Someone who is afraid to be vulnerable may want to connect more than anything else in the world, but the fear of being that exposed holds them back. Not the greatest way to get through life. By not being intimate with someone, you never really let yourself be known, and you will never really know yourself.

We create a lot of who we are based on the reactions of others. When it's someone we're in love with, those reactions govern a large percentage of how we behave. We will share parts of ourselves with someone we love because there is a real desire to connect.

Couples who have truly intimate relationships can't wait to share their days and dreams with each other. They want to connect, and not just in the bedroom. Couples who choose to engage in an intimate relationship, and it is a choice, do so because they want closeness on all levels. In fact a case can be made that intimacy itself is a great aphrodisiac. Most people are more romantic with someone they feel safe with than with a person they don't really know.

Dedicating some time to going deeper and sharing all your needs, hopes, and fears will lead you to feeling that there's at least one person on this planet who cares and who totally gets you. Now that's intimacy.

If the idea of intimacy entices you, while at the same time it causes you to put your guard up, here's something you can do to help yourself open up.

♡ *Talk with the one you love about how being vulnerable makes you feel. This is really the best place to start. Choose a time and place where you and your partner are both comfortable and feeling especially affectionate. Finding the right words may be daunting, so you can begin by asking your partner for help.*

For example, you can ask your partner in advance to respond in a certain way if you start to feel especially vulnerable as you are talking. A code word or hand gesture can signal that you need a hug, some space, or just some patience from your partner while you emote. You may want your partner to listen to you without saying anything, or you may want your partner to interrupt you with questions. It's up to you.

As a way of beginning, you can talk about how closeness makes you feel. Does it make you want to burst into tears or run away and hide? Does it make you angry? Was there something that happened to you in the past that makes being close especially scary? If so, you can choose to talk about this as well. By just saying the words that are in your heart, you will feel a little more trust and a little less fear.

Now ask your partner to share his or her feelings about closeness. We all have them and knowing that you aren't the only one will help the two of you feel closer and give you the sense of intimate connection that you need to continue growing together.

Making It Work

$\mathcal{I}$f you didn't have a close relationship with your primary caretakers as a child, you may find it difficult to form and maintain solid intimate relationships as an adult. Being your own person while also being a loving mate can be a challenge.

It is equally true that, even if you didn't get good parenting or haven't been successful in love, you can become close and stay close to someone who moves you. You can have a dynamite relationship. It comes down to getting really good at taking what you've got and making it work.

There comes a time when, no matter how heinous your parents were, you have to find a way to deal with it and move on. People who spend too much time blaming their parents for where they are in their lives don't have enough energy left to move forward. If your parents didn't give you the security you needed while growing up, you can create the security you need now. You can do this by making good choices.

Perhaps the most important choice is to keep your eye on the future instead of dwelling on the past. This means learning to deal with some uncomfortable emotions. It also may mean learning to deal with people who make you uncomfortable.

Having goals can help you fully enjoy your life, even if you've had a rough start. Each time you hit a new milestone, your self-esteem grows, along with your ability to accomplish more. Many people who have overcome humble or humiliating beginnings are fulfilled in their lives.

Following a dream with your love, like acting in a community theater production or sailing to Hawaii, can help to fill the hole created by a loveless childhood. It's also healthy to have something to look forward to. It can be your yearly vacation or your eventual retirement. I suggest having something on the horizon that floats your boat and, at least once a month, doing something significant to get there.

You may find it inspiring to read the life stories of individuals who have had to deal with the adversity of parents who weren't there for them. Knowing that others have achieved great things can give you strength and some ideas for how to do it yourself.

Even if you never got the love you needed, you can have the life and the relationships you want. It takes patience, persistence, and the ability to give what you want to get. So don't stop trying, and know that you deserve to be loved just for being who you are.

Here are some ways to help you make it work.

♡ *Share your stories of difficult times with your mate. Let your partner comfort you. If you want to, you can even let him or her know exactly how you'd like to be comforted. Talk about how those difficult times made you the person you are now: the person your mate loves.*

♡ *Create a ritual around letting go of those hard times that sometimes fill you with resentment or anger. Write, draw, sculpt, sing, or dance about your difficult experience. Then visualize all your hurt, anger, resentment, and fear about that situation disappearing.*

♡ *Ask your partner to share a challenging experience or situation that has affected him or her. Discuss how the difficulties your partner has endured may have contributed to the qualities you love in her or him.*

Panning for Gold

*I*t has been said that we get to appreciate things in life three times: as anticipation, as the actual event, and as the memory.

Remember how you felt before your first date or that time you skydived? How many hours of sleep have you not minded losing when the next day offered some excitement? It's moments like these that we want to save in the hard-drives of our psyches.

Some would say that anticipation is the best part of anything worthwhile. Personally, I find the planning almost as much fun as the party.

When we finally get to engage in an activity that we treasure or share a fun time with those we love, we are fully living life. That special evening we've been waiting for, or seeing someone we've been thinking about all day, gives us extra energy, and it also gives us something wonderful to look back on.

Our memories are what create the maps of our lives. Feeling good about who we are, the people we're with, and what we have done is what inspires us to do our best every day. If we all could focus on creating positive recollections, the world in general, and our lives in specific, would be much nicer.

It also makes sense that just as we get to experience the joyful moments of our lives three times, the converse is also true: we also have to endure the anticipation, the experience, and the memories of traumatic incidents.

But you can take an active role in making these events less painful than they could be. If you're forced to have a difficult conversation with your love, for example, you can strive to do it in a way that will make you feel good about yourself. When you look back on your life, you'll want to have positive memories about your actions and the people you shared them with.

Think of it as panning for gold. If you let go of the things that are less valuable to you, you'll be left with more positive thoughts floating through your mind. You will remember that you discussed things in an appropriate manner, and everybody involved was uplifted by the experience.

Understanding the stages of how you process events can assist you in making choices that keep your heart fuller and your head freer.

Here are some additional tips to help you separate the wheat from the chaff.

♡ *Instead of flipping on the tube after dinner, ask your partner to sit down and talk about the last time he or she felt miffed* at you and didn't tell you because "it was no biggie" and he or she "got over it." I know this sounds like you're asking for trouble, but the truth is that you are actually preventing trouble. Invest ten minutes in listening to your partner's pain, and neither of you will have to endure an eventual eruption.

I suggest only one of you share on any given day because that way you can take in what the other is saying at a deeper level. Your partner will understand. You can take your turn at a later date, but don't forget you have a turn coming. Little resentments build up over time, and having the opportunity to release one every now and then will keep your intimacy on a positive track.

♡ After your next encounter with a couple treating each other poorly or just acting irritated with one another, talk about how being around them made you feel (rather than just commenting on the bad behavior). And ask your partner how it made him or her feel. This is a great exercise to do on the drive home, and it will help the two of you avoid making the same errors. Discussing your reactions can help to create more positive and more intimate interactions of your own. Be sure to use common sense and let your partner know if you've been triggered by what you experienced. Set boundaries about not projecting your own emotions onto your partner by mistake, and if you find yourselves starting to escalate, make it a ground rule that you will stop immediately and refocus on what works in your relationship instead of what didn't work for your friends.

♡ *Invite your partner to spend an evening reminding each other of some of the favorite times you've shared as a couple. Break out some old photos or watch your wedding video. Reminiscing like this may inspire you to renew your vows, make love, shed tears of joy about days gone by, or it may just leave both of you with a deeper sense of connection and a loving glow.*

Ten New (and Potentially Bold) Exercises to Enhance Your Intimacy

*M*uch of what life and love have to offer is old hat. Truth is that there are only eighty-eight keys on the piano. It's how we play them that makes a melody new. Invite your partner to do some of the following intimate exercises with you. They will enhance your connection and make love fun again.

1. *Mirror exercises.*
   Stand side by side and look into the mirror and simultaneously into your lover's eyes. Mirrors increase light by about 30 percent, and so you will see deeper into the soul of the one you love. You will also be seen in a way that you never

have before. So exhale and get ready to feel the closeness.

2. *Backwards hug.*

Stand back-to-back and hold hands. Now, just feel your partner from this new perspective. Talk about what sensations you have and what emotions come up. Just a few minutes is enough to get to know another side of your partner. Enjoy the uniqueness of the experience.

3. *Alien lover.*

Pretend that your lover is from another planet and doesn't understand anything about life and love on planet Earth, and it is your job to teach him or her. You cannot speak; only gestures and looks are allowed. Let it go wherever you want, as long as you both feel comfortable and are having fun.

4. *The un-plan.*

Plan to get up one weekend morning and go somewhere that neither of you has previously chosen. Just get in the car, flip a coin, and pick a direction to drive. Then, when you find something that looks interesting, stop in and check it out. Have lunch and keep on going if you like, but try to take a different route home. It's all about creating a new experience together.

5. See me.

Blind people touch faces to get a tactile portrait of what someone looks like. Close your eyes and, one at a time, touch each other's faces. Talk about what it was like touching your lover's face and what it felt like being touched. I believe you'll see each other in a new light.

6. Future visualization.

Sit facing each other, hold hands, close your eyes, and each of you picture your future together. Do this for three or four minutes and then open your eyes and share what you saw. Then do it again, but this time use your partner's images and then share where that took you. This exercise can offer amazing insights into what you both want for yourselves and each other.

7. Casual touching.

Anytime you pass each other in the house, extend a hand and touch one another. It can be a high five or a sensual stroke on the small of your back as you slide by your lover in the hallway. Doing this will enhance your emotional intimacy and inspire greater physical closeness.

8. Spot chasing.

On the next pleasant evening when there are spotlights in the sky, follow one to its source.

Many times these are used to bring people to the opening of a new store, but sometimes they announce a grand event, and you may see some things that will create a nice memory.

9. *Surprise, surprise.*
Anticipation can be the best part of a surprise. Tell your mate to mark the calendar for a specific weekend months in advance, but don't tell him or her why. Make reservations at a B&B, and even if it's only for one night, whisk your lover away for a night of sweet romance.

10. *Write right.*
Write your partner a poem and read it to her or him or write a song and sing it. Don't worry about your abilities as a poet or a singer; it's your action that will make it a number-one hit.

These are some new ways to make your relationship sweeter and deeper. As you read this book, feel free to add to the tips or give them your own personal spin. The only way you can fail is not to give it a try.

Ten Tips for Sweetening Your Relationship

Sometimes the idea of trying new things with your partner can seem daunting. The truth is that doing things differently will not only keep your relationship healthy; it will also stimulate your mind and heart. Here are some more tips for making your relationship the best it can be.

1. Let go of the past.

Holding on to the pains of yesterday won't allow you to forgive your partner or yourself and will keep your relationship from reaching the next level. Forgiveness is really a gift you give to yourself.

2. *Create your fantasy vacation.*

   Even if you don't have the time or the money for a vacation right now, planning for one may be just what you need to inspire yourselves. Looking at travel brochures and talking about what you'd like to do can give you a little lift. Creating the dream is the beginning of making it come true.

3. *Take a class together.*

   Try CPR (and hope you never need it), cooking, dancing, golf, or tennis. Learning something new together will make you both feel more connected and help you discover parts of your relationship that may have been hidden.

4. *Give each other a makeover.*

   Go to the mall and pick out some items that you would like to see one another wear. The fashion show itself will be a blast. Have fun with it.

5. *Remember why you fell in love in the first place.*

   Returning to that moment will help you appreciate where you are with each other now. If you can, go back to the place you first met and relive your first date.

6. *Have lunch together once a week.*

Think of it as a daytime date. Many couples don't get to visit each other during the day. If you can do it, having lunch together on a regular basis will add a positive dimension to your relationship.

7. *Do the unusual.*

Enjoy the full moon, throw a costume/theme party, or visit an orchid farm. Thinking outside the box can make your relationship phenomenal.

8. *Do the lazy weekend thing.*

Pick a day and just hang out with the newspaper and the one you love. Spend a day as human beings rather than human doings. It's amazing how revitalizing lazy days can be (and I realize this is the exact opposite of tip number 7).

9. *Ask each other twenty questions.*

Do you know your love's favorite movie? How about his or her favorite song? Does your love know yours? There are probably a few hundred facts about your partner that you are unaware of, and vice versa. Asking each other about these things will make both of you feel cared for and bring you closer.

10. *Make the normal days extra special.*

Create special moments. Leave your partner a love note on the fridge, in the shower, or in a jacket pocket where you know your sweetheart will reach. Send your partner a card at work or leave a loving/sexy phone message.

As the years go by, the memory of your sweetest moments will tell your love story in a way that nothing else can.

PART
2

Intimate

Conversations

Three Conversations

*H*ow often do you and your partner feel that neither of you is getting what the other is saying? It's almost as if the two of you were having different discussions. It amazes me how differently two people can perceive a conversation, but the truth is that this is a natural thing and we all do it.

When the two of you are talking, there are three distinct dialogues going on at the same time: the one you think you're having, the one your partner thinks you're having, and the one that is really occurring. We don't correctly hear what someone else is saying to us because we have our own listening filters that cause us to put our own interpretation on what the other person is saying, rather than hearing what they're actually saying.

Perhaps we may have some strong emotions in play or may be busy thinking about our response. At times, we can be distracted by outside influences, like the television, or internal ones, such as our previous histories, insecurities, or even how we are feeling physically.

All of these things combined can create the perfect conversational storm: a place where nobody feels heard and both parties end up floundering in a sea of misunderstanding.

If you'd like to still the waters and have calm communication, start by realizing that you may not be as clear as your partner needs you to be. Yes, I know that he or she has equal responsibility here, but someone has to get things started, so why not seize the opportunity and open up the topic?

Begin the process by telling your partner about an issue you'd like to discuss, letting him or her know that you want the conversation to strengthen the relationship. Then speak your feelings, stopping after each point so you can both really hear what was just said. Then, as your partner repeats back his or her interpretation of your words, be sure to gently clarify any misunderstandings. Keep doing this for each point until you feel that your partner understands what you're trying to say. It may seem a bit cumbersome, but by going slowly through this process, you eliminate misinterpretation.

After you've been heard, allow your partner to respond. After each point, repeat what you heard your partner say, and make sure she or he clarifies anything you may have misunderstood. Extend the extra effort to make sure that neither of you filters out important points or blocks feelings. This kind of open communication will make for smooth sailing in your relationship.

Here's an example:

Him: I believe we have a good relationship, and I have a thought that might help to make it great.

Her: Okay. Let me have it.

Him: When I come to you with something that's bothering me, sometimes I feel that you're not really listening and letting me in. Now, what did you just hear me say?

Her: I hear you saying that I don't let you in.

Him: I also said that sometimes it seems like you aren't really listening; perhaps it's when you're momentarily distracted, but I don't feel heard.

Her: Oh, I get it. Sometimes I'm not really tuned in while you're speaking. Is that right?

Him: Exactly, and I'd just like you to make the effort, and I'd like us to continue to do this, to repeat back to each other what we hear each other saying, when we talk about serious issues so that we both feel connected by our conversation.

Her: Honey, that may be the most romantic thing you've ever said to me. And I will gladly continue to do that when we have deep conversations.

If your partner doesn't want to participate, give him or her some time, and just use the techniques yourself. Yes, it will be awkward, but most people learn best through example. There are many couples whose communication breaks down on a regular basis, and somehow these couples muddle through, at least temporarily. If your partner continues to stonewall you, professional help is usually just a phone call away.

Learning how to identify your filters and working to keep your conversations as clear as possible will never fail you. No matter how difficult the subject matter, dedicate yourself to talking it through. If you and your partner can both do this, you will give your relationship the best tool possible: good communication.

Asking the right questions will assist you in gaining clarity. Here are some questions you can ask to get to a deeper level of understanding.

♡ *Ask yourself these questions: How am I feeling about what my partner just said? How are my feelings getting in the way of me hearing the words? Do my feelings remind me of a past experience, relationship, or time in my life?*

Here are some questions to ask your partner: What do you want to change about this situation? What's the most important thing you want me to know about this situation? How can I help the situation?

Consider This

$\mathscr{I}$f you want to preserve your intimacy and deepen it, it's best to speak your thoughts and feelings to your partner. Yet sometimes this is hard, especially if you're asking your partner to look at the other side of an argument or to do something differently. How many spouses choose to be silent for years rather than ask their partner to take on more responsibility in household chores? I don't know the percentage, but it must be high.

How do you ask your mate to set the table or miss a game or return to cooking after a decade-long hiatus?

Rather than engaging in valuable communication, some people deal with their negative feelings by giving others the silent treatment. But clamming up, quietly fuming, or staring down another person is about as productive as trying to put out a fire with gasoline.

If you're hurt or angry, holding it in is unhealthy for you and your partner. To overcome this stress-inducing behavior, start by asking yourself what you hope to gain by continuing to be silent. Common sense dictates that if you have a goal or a game plan, communicating will help you get there.

Funny thing is, most problems are easily solved if you just kindly and honestly discuss what's on your mind. The key lies in the delivery. Remember that wise old saying, "It's not what you say but how you say it"? Speaking with a soft voice and choosing words that are not inflammatory will help. But other steps are sometimes necessary, especially if you want someone to go above and beyond what he or she might consider the call of duty.

People will usually only do what they want to do or have to do unless you make it worth their while.

Here's a revolutionary suggestion: simply ask your loved one to "Please consider [insert your request here], and let me know how you feel about it when you're comfortable." Be very clear that you don't want an answer right away. Thinking about it and even discussing it can also be important steps.

Here's an example. Every evening when Barney comes home, his wife Betty has dinner waiting. Barney loves that she takes care of him in this way (feeding a man is very nurturing and enhances intimacy), but he feels rushed to sit down and eat with her. He'd actually prefer to have a few minutes to wash his face and change into some comfortable clothes.

Barney: Honey, I love that you make dinner for us almost every night. It's truly a gift, and I am very grateful. I would like you to please consider one minor adjustment. Could you time it so that I can have a few minutes to freshen up before we sit down? [Using girl-speak by saying "freshen up" will help Betty understand his needs better.] You don't need to give me an answer now. Just think about it and let me know.

Betty: Barney, you know how much I love my routines, but thanks for asking so nicely, and I'll sleep on it.

The following evening when Barney comes home, Betty says, "Hi honey. Why don't you go upstairs and take care of yourself and then come down and help me set the table for dinner." She has taken in Barney's request and also found a way to give herself some more time and get some assistance with prep for their evening meal. It's a win-win for this relationship.

What you do by asking your partner to "please consider" your request is take what could be considered a demand and turn it into a choice. This is empowering.

So instead of engaging in a battle of wills because you want your partner to adopt new ideas or behaviors, try this little tool.

Remember, communication deepens your connection with one another; it is the most important part of your relationship. Sharing your life with someone requires that you say what is in your head and your heart. It never hurts to express your positive feelings. A few extra words at the right time can turn a humdrum relationship into a poetic one.

Remember these important tips.

♡ *Once your partner has considered your proposition, accept his or her decision cheerfully. You need to respect the other person's boundaries. Doing so in this case may serve to inspire your partner to do what you'd like after all.*

♡ *If your partner is willing to consider and then accept what you ask, express your gratitude. You can ask your partner if there is anything you can do differently to please him or her, or you can give back to your partner in some other special way. You know best what your mate enjoys, so pick something special. A massage, an evening out, or a lovely meal would be good. You can also do something really different (see chapter 7).*

Avoiding Ugly Arguments

*E*very now and then, even the most loving of couples will get into an argument that may rattle the windows and will definitely rattle the hearts of those involved. Experience dictates that most of the power in these unfortunate encounters comes from unhealthy behaviors.

Check it out. Recall the last time you and your mate argued with each other. Did either or both of you bring up past issues? This is done to deflect responsibility and avoid discomfort. It usually makes the issue worse and may create additional problems.

Instead of getting defensive and escalating, consider these additional tools you can use to keep you from hurting your relationship or shutting down your heart.

♡ *Choose your words carefully. Don't swear or use inflammatory or accusatory language that will make your partner defensive or angry. Instead, say what's on your mind and in* your heart. In the heat of the moment, this can be challenging, but a careful consideration of what is being said can make the difference between a resolution and a battle.

♡ Don't raise your voice. Raising your voice is a form of verbal abuse, and being yelled at can feel like an assault. It can be very frightening for people of all ages and sizes. Try being an adult and sharing your feelings without raising your voice to get your point across. By yelling, what you are really doing is expressing your own pain through anger. Don't do it.

♡ Look into your heart. It may help to ask yourself a few questions. Are you angry at the other person or are you frustrated with the situation? Does this individual deserve your wrath? How would you respond if someone said to you what you are saying to your loved one? Doing a quick evaluation of your true feelings will give you a different perspective and perhaps help you feel your way through the issue rather than see it as a win-lose proposition.

♡ Ask for what you really need. Could your ire have been calmed with an apology or a hug? If so, ask for what you need directly without making a scene. If a conversation or some clarity is needed and you've been stewing for a little while, say so. It's best to be open about your feelings as soon as circumstances permit.

♡ Don't drink and discuss. If alcohol or drugs are involved, you won't be coming from a clear place. If either of you is under the influence, it's best not to try to have any kind of serious communication. It may be hard to remember this rule if you've been sipping martinis all night, so make an agreement with your partner that when you're partying, deep discussions are off limits.

Honey, What's Bugging You?

$\mathcal{A}$re you up to the task? Are you ready to ask your sweetheart the most daring and revealing question you could ever pose?

Okay, here it is: "Honey, is there anything I do that totally bugs you?" By asking this question, you are opening a Pandora's box. You are also creating a vehicle that can propel you both to a lifetime of connected communication, the likes of which is seldom seen in modern relationships.

Not everyone has the ability to pose this question to his or her partner. Having a face-to-face with the one you love is hard enough, but being able to ask for direction (all right, some would call it criticism) is going above and beyond what most couples ever do in intimate conversation.

If you're interested in asking this question, it's a bit like preparing for a marathon. Here is a two-part training exercise to help you get into the proper emotional condition.

Think about who you are and how you behave and what you would change about yourself (if anything). Then put yourself in your partner's shoes and think about what it is your partner would say if you asked what he or she would like to change about you. If you really look at yourself from these two perspectives, the picture you see could inspire you to make some awesome adjustments.

The hard part isn't really the question; it's being able to truly hear your partner's response and being willing to adjust your behavior or habits to make your true love more comfortable. Be prepared to shave your beard or stop buying so many handbags; be willing to be less bubbly at parties or less keyed up while watching ball games.

Making these kinds of changes is a rite of passage in any top-flight relationship. If a certain behavior of yours that you thought was cute or, at the very least, tolerable now grates on your partner like fingernails on a blackboard, I'd think you'd have to want to let it go.

Hey, this is real life, and as we mature, our preferences change. You're so much better off being proactive instead of letting this person you love, and your relationship, suffer because he or she is too kind to tell you what's up.

Whatever the sacrifice, asking is a great way to strengthen your relationship, and making changes will keep your mind sharper. Finding a way to debug your relationship before any real damage is done can also save you years of grief.

I've seen too many couples on the therapy couch because their problems escalated due to a behavior their other half was not all that attached to. Many times, couples, with their jaws dropping, say to their mate, "Why didn't you ever tell me that before? I'm totally fine with letting it go."

So take the risk and give your partner the gift that keeps on giving by asking if there's anything you do that bugs him or her. The answer may put you on a merry-go-round for a little while, but if you follow through, the brass ring of a great relationship is yours for the grabbing.

The hardest part of using this tool is getting started. Here are a few tips.

♡ *Ask your partner to read this chapter. This may inspire your partner to start talking to you about his or her pet peeve, without your having to ask.*

♡ *When it's your turn to say what's bugging you, be gentle and keep it short. You want this to be an intimate conversation, not a monologue.*

♡ *Alternatively, write down one thing that bugs you about your partner and ask your partner to do the same. Exchange notes. Take ten minutes to gently discuss your feelings and, if you agree to both change, burn the notes together as a symbol of ending something that wasn't working and starting a new chapter.*

Intimate Apology

There are so many ways to apologize, it's a wonder why some couples so seldom use them. I shake my head in disbelief that something so simple and so helpful to intimate relationships can be so underutilized.

It's as if we only had a limited number of ways to say "I'm sorry" in our vocabulary. Last time I checked, it was next to impossible to run out of words. Why then is this healing response so seldom used?

Some people refuse to say they are sorry for anything. It seems as though saying "I'm sorry" is akin to saying "I'm wrong." Mistakes are human, and when one person makes an error that unintentionally injures another, the polite thing to do is to apologize. If you stepped on a stranger's toe, you'd say, "Oops, I'm so sorry," but if you say or do something that rubs your partner the wrong way, are you as forthcoming with offering amends?

Being unable to admit mistakes hurts your partner, yourself, and your relationship. If your partner is unwilling or unable to apologize, the key may be to confront his or her insecurity or pride in a nonthreatening way. This is important to do, because if hurt feelings are left hanging, it's bad for your connection.

The problem with not being able to express remorse to your partner is that your partner will start to feel that you don't care. Trust me, we all say and do stupid things (I personally have a master's degree in this). So the next time you put your foot in your mouth, show that you're not a heel, and make an apology that comes from your soul. It will be a big step forward in your relationship.

There are numerous ways to express your heartfelt sorrow without groveling or making you feel that you are compromising your integrity.

♡ *If your partner has trouble apologizing, try saying something like "Have you ever noticed that saying 'I'm sorry' is a bit difficult for you?" Ask your partner if he or she loves you enough to work on being a little more sensitive.*

♡ *Here are some fun phrases that can help you say what you mean without feeling like a complete idiot:*

"Sorry, for a moment I was taken over by aliens."

"I don't know what I was thinking. My brain froze. I apologize."

"Oops. I just turned into my third-grade teacher. Sorry."

As long as it's not overused, apologizing with a little self-deprecating humor can prevent some of the onus that may come from this valuable act of contrition. But if all your apologies are out of Seinfeld, then you may not get the response you want. It's also always wise to remember that actions speak louder than words.

Ten Tips for Building Empathy

*P*erhaps your best tool for creating intimate conversations and deepening your relationship is your ability to feel empathy. The good news is that you don't have to go to graduate school to learn how to use it. We are all capable of finding that place within ourselves where we can make our partner feel that she or he is not alone.

Here are ten things to help guide you in using empathy.

E—Empathy means to feel what your partner is feeling. Put yourself in your partner's shoes (or high heels). It will give you a new perspective and help you better understand how the other person ticks.

M—Manage any upset. You can't feel what your partner is feeling if your emotions are high. Find a way to calm yourself before you try to engage in a meaningful conversation. Taking a few deep breaths and realizing that it's not about you is a great way to begin.

P—Partnership consciousness is key to having an empathetic dialogue in a relationship. Remember, you are in this with someone who loves you. It makes it much easier to deal with any problems when you feel you are on the same team.

A—Anticipate a positive outcome. This will help you focus on solving your relationship issues rather than creating new ones. Allow for the tears and the fears, but keep your heart focused on the future and healing. Focusing on the positive will help you be there for your partner.

T—Truthfulness is paramount when you are working toward balance and harmony. Talk about everything you are feeling and don't hold back. Just remember to do it with kindness. Truthfulness builds the energy between you and allows you to totally trust each other's feelings.

H—Healing is at the core of empathy. The process is one of soothing the other person's pain as well as your own. Keep your focus on this dynamic, and you will achieve your desired outcome.

E—Emotional connection is the greatest resource you have. Hold your partner's hands or, if appropriate, embrace warmly to show you care. Connecting this way allows for a greater flow of empathy.

$\mathcal{T}$—Trust your feelings. Yoda knew that feelings were the key to answering any question or finding a way out of any disaster. It worked for Luke Skywalker, and it can work for you.

$\mathcal{I}$—Integrity can be a powerful partner in creating an empathetic connection with someone. Show your integrity. If there is any outside or selfish agenda, no one will grow or heal.

$\mathcal{C}$—Compassion is the constant companion of empathy. Wanting the other person to feel better, even if it isn't toward you, is the essence of this gift. Show your compassion fully and completely. This tool will serve you well throughout your life.

You don't have to go far to find empathy. It is a gift that is given to all who have the willingness to look within at the goodness and sensitivity we are naturally blessed with.

PART
3

Intimate

Space

The Morning Ritual

$\mathcal{I}$t's amazing how powerfully connecting it can be to sit with your mate in the morning. Hanging out together, sharing breakfast or a cup of coffee with your loved one, can be one of the most bonding experiences you ever have. This little ritual has become one of my favorite times of the day.

I completely understand how easy it can be to avoid or ignore this moment of togetherness. With the hustle and bustle of getting ready for the day, finding a moment to spend quality time with your partner can be easily forgotten, but at what cost?

I think of moments like these as emotional vitamin supplements. Taking a few minutes to make sure my partner has the support she needs to get through the day with a full heart is an important and valuable action.

It's very painful to be at work, school, or even at home and not feel connected to the one you love. This is especially true if there are any issues still brewing from the night before. We have all heard stories of people who left the house in a bad mood and, tragically, never returned because they were killed in an accident. These things do happen, and there may be nothing more tormenting than to know that the last words you said to the one you loved were harsh. For this and so many other reasons, it's important to connect with your partner in a positive way each and every day. And it can't help but deepen your intimacy.

Making that connection is one of the easiest things on earth, as long as you don't let the morning rush or your desire to look perfect get in the way. Even if a morning meal is not part of your routine, or you're more inclined to chow down on an energy bar on your way to work, or you've sworn off caffeine, there are many ways to touch your partner's heart without taking a lot of time.

A moment of tenderness with your loved one will strengthen you for the day ahead. Don't leave home in the morning without it.

Here are some tips to help you make the morning ritual a joy.

♡ *Give your partner a ten-second hug and kiss before you leave the house in the morning and when you return at night.*

♡ *Put a special little note in your partner's pocket, handbag, or backpack to remind him or her of your love.*

♡ If you're running late, touch base with your partner on the phone as you each go to your respective destinations.

♡ Try being an early bird and wake your partner with a kiss and some juice or coffee.

Sharing the Bathroom

$\mathcal{R}$elationships can be made in the bedroom, but they can be shattered in the bathroom. I have seen the need to share one toilet bring a number of couples to the breaking point. It can also create some resentment if your partner is primping when you have an urgent need to use the facilities.

To keep your romance alive, I recommend using separate bathrooms if possible. Several studies have noted that happiness in a home can be in direct proportion to the number of bathrooms available. The more bathrooms, the more joy and the more intimacy.

For those in one-bath abodes, this could be gloomy news. But you must get creative in order to thrive. I suggest you and your partner get really good at timing. Many happy partners who share the bathroom have worked out a system that could rival a Space Shuttle launch at Cape Canaveral.

Using a small bathroom at the same time takes as much dexterity as the winning steps on *Dancing with the Stars*. Stretching up as your partner bends down, grabbing your toothbrush as your other half reaches for a razor, is an artistic piece of choreography.

I know some couples who have motor homes or trailers in the driveway and will make use of the spare bathroom when the need arises. Some men resort to "watering the flowers" when their better half has the "occupied" sign on the bathroom door. It can seem like a reasonable alternative, unless you happen to live in a condo complex or are in Duluth and it's January.

For some couples, sharing the bathroom is an intimate experience. It's where they start their days, plan their lives, and deepen their connection. For those with busy lives, it may be the only one-to-one time they get on a regular basis.

Bottom line here is that if you and your partner can have separate bathrooms, it may be a way of reducing your stress and increasing some of the mystery that may have gotten lost in your romance. If your lifestyle requires that you learn to share, it can teach you how to deal with each other under the most intimate of circumstances.

Here are some tips for sharing a bathroom with the one you love.

♡ *Bathe or shower together. This is perhaps the most intimate and fun way of sharing the bathroom. It could be the most romantic ten minutes of your daylight hours, and it will keep you thinking about each other. Bathing together has the added benefit of saving water and energy.*

♡ *Take ten minutes to clean things up in the way you know your partner will like. Wipe down the counter and sink—even if it's only water, it will take thirty seconds and your partner will appreciate it. Bathroom countertops can be another area of contention. It's usually easier to deal with organization than with chaos, so I suggest deferring to the partner who requests neatness.*

♡ *Be a man (if you're the man). If you have the option, give up the master bath and use the other bathroom, giving your mate as much space as possible. This is an act of caring. It is one of those nonverbal ways a guy can say "I love you," and for some women, it's a better gift than diamonds.*

Relationship Lunch

*M*ost of us think more about what we want for lunch than about what we want for our relationship. Have you ever considered what your relationship would be like with, say, an extra helping of mutual respect, or how about supersizing it with deep, heartfelt communication? The possibilities are as varied as a deli menu.

Most of us go into a relationship believing that we know what we want. It's a type of hunger that can only be sated by that certain someone. After a while, though, we may find that what we craved has become a bit bland, and we may desire something a little different to give the relationship that extra kick. The good news is that even if you've been living together for years, you can always discover something new and wonderful about your partner.

Unfortunately, some people think that the thing to do is to dine at another restaurant. This can be bad for your digestion because the new waiters won't treat you as well and the new chef has no idea of how you like your eggs cooked. To paraphrase the old Pillsbury commercial, nothin' says lovin' like somethin' from *your* oven.

Take the time to think about how to be in your relationship and what you really want from life and your partner. Doing this with your partner is a way of getting closer and will give both of you more of what you really need. The process of sharing your desires with your mate is a very intimate act. Why not do it over a romantic lunch?

Adding some flavor is as easy as adding a pinch of salt to your favorite dish. Here are a few tips to make your time together a tasty treat.

♡ *Do something together that you have never done before. This can be as simple as going out of town for a weekend or something as exotic as taking the Orient Express. Make some plans. It will give you something to look forward to, and the adventure will create wonderful memories.*

♡ *Do a life swap. If you have friends who live in a different state, consider trading homes for a week. This way you get to experience an entirely new way of living. It may fill you with gratitude for what you have or inspire you to set new goals. I suggest you take a video camera along—who knows? It might turn into a reality TV show.*

♡ *Rearrange the furniture. As simple as this may sound, it will actually create a different energy in your home. Just moving a few things around can have an impact on how you see your life and your partner. It's also fun to sleep in another room of your house. Both of these activities will add a new dimension to your relationship.*

Pre-Bedtime Bonding

One of the most fascinating differences between men and women is their pre-sleep patterns. Men go to bed, and women "get ready" to go to bed. I don't have an exact count, but there must be at least a couple of dozen individual steps that many women take before they get under the covers.

Yes, there are a million or so metrosexual guys who use a face moisturizer, but the vast majority don't go even that far. Most men simply brush their teeth, put on their pajamas (or not), and hit the pillow.

A woman's sleep-prep pattern is a more ritualistic process, not unlike the care taken in creating a master work of art. It is a way to pay homage to the day's end and an affirmation that tomorrow will be brighter. It is also a way of adding some special touches to a potential night of lovemaking.

I believe that there is something therapeutic to this dance. Removing makeup at the end of the day is a way of casting off the old and smoothing the rough spots. Taking a bath before bed is not just relaxing; it is restorative. Allowing the stress of the day to simply drift away as you soak in warm water is healing. The act of putting on lotions is a way of saying "I'm worth the effort." It's empowering to know that you've done things to make yourself look and feel better, and the time a woman takes to care of herself is usually returned tenfold. The man in her life benefits from the results as well.

Maybe this is one of the reasons women outlive their male counterparts. It does make a man wonder—and perhaps want to take a second look at the men's skin care products the next time he's out shopping.

Women take the time to primp, powder, and perfume because it makes them feel better about themselves, which alone can add years to your life and life to your years. I'm not suggesting that all guys should get manicures, and I don't picture most men leaving the office, saying "I can't wait to slip into a bubble bath." But we guys do need to consider how a little more low-key self-care could help us feel better and enhance our intimacy.

Most guys simply don't have a clue about how to begin, and it doesn't feel so macho to ask your significant other to recommend a good eye cream. To avoid this dilemma, some men actually "borrow" their loved one's products. (Funny as it may sound, this has been an issue in therapy for a number of couples.) This should be a clue for one of you to ask if you can help, or help yourself.

So the next time you're impatiently waiting for the love of your life to come to bed, just remember that she (or he) is doing something to make both of your lives longer and lovelier.

Here are some things you can do with your partner to increase your bedtime bonding.

♡ Create a romantic ritual, like taking a bath together at least once a week. It is a great intimacy booster. At times when you're not in the mood for romance, simply running a shower or bath for the one you love is a caring act that your partner will appreciate. You can also try setting out each other's PJs, lighting candles, or just warming up the bed for your honey.

♡ The next time you need to go to the drugstore, do it with your partner. That way your feminine half can tell your masculine half what lotion to buy, and he can share his preference for aromatic shampoos with her. It's a great way to learn a little more about your partner and perhaps yourself.

♡ Make it part of your regular nighttime routine to check the house together, making sure the doors are locked, the animals are fed, and the kids are sleeping soundly, before you go to bed. It will help you both sleep more comfortably and is an act of togetherness.

Ten Tips for a Closer Relationship

*G*ood relationships almost never just happen. They usually are a combination of hard work, honest communication, and going the extra mile to add a little magic.

Here are ten tools that long-term successful couples use to make their relationships work.

1. Talk about and plan for the future.
Goals are important to your overall happiness. Having a contingency plan in case of an emergency will allow you to enjoy your time with your partner more thoroughly.

2. Compliment your mate.

Kind words given at the right time are fuel for the future to those who are fortunate enough to receive them. Giving compliments to the one you love helps keep you connected.

3. Ask questions.

Show interest in what your other half is doing by asking about his or her day and how he or she is feeling about things. This will make your partner feel you care and open the door to deeper conversation.

4. Be considerate of your partner's feelings.

Making a joke at someone else's expense always stings the other person. Name-calling is downright insulting. If you engage in this dangerous game, stop while you still have someone to play with.

5. Take care of the business side of your relationship.

Money is the cause of nearly one-third of all divorces. If you're having financial issues, get some professional help to get back on track.

6. **Be accountable for your actions.**

If you screw up, admit it, and apologize if an apology is called for. Keep your word and know that trust is something that is continually earned.

7. **Give emotional support.**

Emotional support may be the single most valuable component in a relationship. Having someone in your corner while you navigate through your problem de jour is a gift of the highest order.

8. **Stay connected physically.**

Holding hands, exchanging foot rubs, giving your partner an unexpected hug—these moments are as important as making love. One day they will be more important.

9. **Remember to be polite.**

Even if you're offended for the moment, it's always best to keep your anger in check. As soon as an opportunity arises to discuss what happened, take it. You don't want to hold on to anything that you don't have to hold on to. You may also find that if you wait an hour or two, the issues (or at least the anger) will go away.

10. *Keep your mind and heart open.*

People change. If one day your partner takes up transcendental meditation or changes political parties, you need to be open-minded enough to go with the flow. Make an agreement that, no matter what, you will still love each other.

Using any one of these tools will help keep your relationship more peaceful and make you more desirable. Using several on a regular basis will give you a sense of joy that you may never have experienced before.

PART
4

Intimate

Differences

Releasing the Need to Control

Some people mistakenly feel that once they commit to a relationship, they have been granted permission to oversee and control every detail of their partner's existence. To borrow a phrase from Porgy and Bess, "That ain't necessarily so."

Intimacy increases with mutual respect. And if you respectfully request rather than demand your partner's opinion or help, you are more likely to get what you want.

To avoid the natural backlash that comes with inappropriate actions, you need to take a close look at how you get your needs met, what the words mean to you, and how your partner may hear them differently.

I know this sounds like a long process, especially if your motivation is just to get your other half to bring home a carton of milk. But if you take it to heart, you may eliminate a large percentage of your arguments, hurt feelings, and thoughts of using a roll of duct tape to keep your loved one's mouth shut.

Relationships are called partnerships for a reason. Unless the two of you agree that you want one person to have all the control, neither of you has the right to make the other subservient. There is a sound psychological reason for this. If you don't treat each other as equals, the love can't flow equally, and if that isn't happening, you are eventually going to question the relationship.

Keeping your vocal tones within human comfort zones, staying emotionally available, and simply being kind will make your partner want to be more available to you. I implore you to ask your mate what she or he is experiencing. Yes, it's a risk, but you might want to ask your partner if some of your behavior feels controlling and, if so, what she or he would like you to change. It may be hard to hear, but if you do it now, you'll save yourself future grief. Changing your behavior is not as tough as you think, because all behavior is a choice.

Working together is one of the best parts of a relationship. The give and take is a dance that would put Fred and Ginger to shame. Having your requests granted with a smile may only be a matter of changing a few words, adjusting your tone, and perhaps your attitude.

You'll get the most out of your life together if you treat your partner with the same respect you'd ask for yourself. This is not rocket science, but it's a discovery that could make your relationship as bright as any star.

Here are some tips to help you create more balance in your relationship.

♡ *Turn your demands into requests. Doing this gives your partner an opportunity to exercise his or her free will, which is empowering. The chances of getting your needs met are much higher if your partner feels like he or she has some choice in the matter. So the next time you ask your partner to do something for you, make sure you phrase it as a request, not a demand. Instead of "Get me a carton of milk when you go to the store," try saying "Honey, when you're out, could you please pick me up a carton of milk?"*

♡ *Write down the top three things you feel controlling about in your relationship. Think about what you usually say or do, and write down an alternate strategy that doesn't seek to control or put down your partner. Make a commitment to try out your alternate strategies the next time you get the chance.*

♡ *The next time you feel controlled or put down by your partner when he or she asks you to do something, immediately help your partner rephrase the request, so it feels more respectful. Then respond positively. Doing so will reinforce your partner's behavior, and the interaction will open both of you up. Take a few minutes to discuss what just happened, and talk about it for just five minutes again the following day. This is how intimate relationships are created.*

Are You the Cat
or the Bunny?

Say that your partner just keeps going and going, and you're more of a "cat person" who likes to take naps and hang out around the house. How can the two of you live in harmony and give each other the space and companionship you need to be personally happy as well as content in your relationship?

I believe that differences make for good relationships; however, certain behaviors can cause imbalance and create distress. To make your particular differences work for you, take a good look at your own energy level and how it might affect your connection. Once you understand your own behavior preferences and your partner's, you can begin to find ways to balance things out.

If you are an Energizer bunny, do your best not to think that your cat-person partner is lazy or that he or she doesn't want to play with you. Cat people need to understand that "going" is the way Energizer bunnies relax. Talk with your partner about your differences. Encouraging your partner to go with your flow will be much easier once you have a mutual understanding.

First, recognize that some people get more energy by resting and others increase their energy through activity. If both of you can accept this, then you can plan your lives so you are both at your best. Realize also that everyone's rhythms can change over time. Differences in activity levels will usually shift over the years. I know people who took up marathon running late in life and others who left careers as professional athletes to write.

Realize that you don't have to do everything together to be a successful couple. Participating doesn't mean that you have to be attached at the hip. It's more a matter of sharing the experience in some way versus feeling left out or being pushed in a direction that's uncomfortable for you.

Finally, trust that eventually both of you will get what you want and need. You will enjoy your life with your partner more if you do.

So the next time your cat person wants to take a snooze in the sun and you want to do some running around, show how you appreciate your differences and your mate by picking up something special... like extra batteries.

Here are some tips to help you make the cat purr and the bunny hop.

- ♡ *It's helpful to let your mate know what you want. If your partner usually falls asleep as soon as his or her head hits the pillow, and you want to kiss and cuddle tonight, make sure you say you've got some romantic intentions before the lights go out.*

- ♡ *If you tend to run out of batteries in the evening and the two of you have plans for dinner and a movie, I suggest that you take a nap in the afternoon. This way, you will have more energy for your sweetheart at night.*

Early Birds and Night Owls

*C*an two people who have vastly differing waking and sleeping patterns find happiness and success in a loving relationship? Of course, but it does take a little creativity to make it work. First, it helps to understand that some people simply have more energy in the morning and others have more energy at night.

For a true night owl, morning people can seem twisted. Putting on running shoes and going for a jog at the crack of dawn is not only an impossible act; it's unthinkable before a second cup of coffee. Some people who claim to be allergic to mornings can find it difficult to even talk with their partners before they completely wake up.

For the early bird, staying up to watch Leno, read the paper, or chitchat about the day's activities may be equally unattainable. An aversion to late nights can also put the kibosh on intimacy.

Our sleeping/waking patterns are called circadian rhythms, which correspond to the Earth's rotation. If you have traveled abroad, you may have experienced your body clock gradually adapting to different time zones. When you were at home, you were in bed by ten, but while in Rome, you were able to party into the wee hours of the morning or had to sleep for an entire day to adjust to the time change. This is because when you travel, you take your rhythm with you.

If you and your partner have opposite tempos, fear not. There is hope. Couples can find many ways to connect, even if their bodies are on different time clocks. It helps to remember that moderation in all things is key to a balanced and intimate relationship.

The night owl may never turn into an early bird or vice versa, but with a few adjustments, the two of you can still build a happy nest. Here are some tips to help you get there.

♡ *Let your partner know that you want more time together. If the two of you want to get into the same rhythm, start by making small adjustments, such as going to bed a little later or waking up a little earlier. This may be easier to do if you begin the process on a long weekend or on vacation.*

♡ *If you have trouble staying up late to play a wild game of Monopoly, try catching a nap at some point during the day. That way you can hang in there and collect some rent on Boardwalk and Park Place.*

♡ *If you're not an early bird, try a little exercise to help you get going in the morning. If you need some aid in relaxing at night, try drinking chamomile or another herbal tea.*

Sleepless in Relationship

*Y*our sleep problems may go beyond night-owl and early-bird dilemmas. According to a survey by the National Sleep Foundation (2008), nearly 20 percent of people in relationships have trouble sleeping with their mate and another 12 percent of married people actually choose to sleep alone. Not sleeping well can affect intimacy, mood, and overall marital satisfaction.

Some of the more common issues that cause sleep distress include blanket and pillow snatching, snoring, body temperature, and conflicts about who gets which side of the bed. Other problems that make sleeping together difficult are teeth grinding, unresolved conflicts, and slumbering with animals or children. Nightmares, sleepwalking, and even unclipped toenails may play a role.

It will come as no surprise that couples with children get less sleep than those with an empty nest, and more than 10 percent of married parents report sleeping with a child. Some do this to comfort the child or to avoid their own separation anxiety, while others use it as a way to avoid emotional closeness with their partner.

Even though some couples know they could sleep better if they were alone, most opt for the intimate comfort of sleeping together. Most of us feel more secure when the one we love is resting by our side. And if you have any serious health issues, having your partner next to you may save your life.

Discussing the problem of physical comfort is going to become more necessary in the years to come, so start getting used to it now. Learning how to sleep better as a couple can take a little time, but the effort is worth it. Waking up in the arms of the one you love is one of the best things in life.

Here are several things you can do to help get a good night's sleep.

♡ *Try spooning with your partner to enhance a blissful night's rest. Spooning is also a great way to stay connected with the one you love.*

♡ *If you sleep with an electric blanket or mattress pad, get one with dual controls (one for each of you). This way if you need to make an adjustment in the middle of the night, you won't roast or freeze your partner. And of course, you get to keep your side exactly how you like it. By the way, cooling as well as heating pads and blankets are now available.*

♡ *Consider buying a better mattress. A bad mattress can be the cause of your sleeplessness. Many beds now have adjustable* firmness controls and even come with heat and massage features.

♡ Snoring affects 30 percent of married couples. There are many over-the-counter treatments that you can try, but snoring can also be a symptom of sleep apnea. If your honey sounds like a moose searching for its mate, have him or her get a checkup.

♡ Avoid working or eating an hour before you go to bed.

♡ If one of you likes the air conditioner kept on at night in the summer and the other doesn't, try opening a window or using a fan instead.

♡ If your partner steals all the covers or pillows, keep a blanket and extra pillow by your side of the bed.

♡ Cuddling is pleasurable for most, but some people can't sleep entwined with their mate. If you or your partner needs space to sleep, try snuggling for twenty minutes before you go into your sleeping pose.

For the Love of Giving

Human beings can be divided into two types: givers and takers. A successful intimate relationship between the two requires finding the right balance. Surely, two givers can have a happy life together. The giver-receiver relationship also works, but for different reasons. Givers want to see the smile on their partner's face when they bestow an offering on the one they love. Whether it's making your loved one a sandwich or buying him or her a car, the act of giving is pleasurable for the giver.

Some couples have this wonderful habit of not only giving to each other but of giving to the community as well. For many in a traditional relationship, the stay-at-home partner also volunteers for a cause both partners support. If you want to contribute to the well-being of humanity and you are working full time, it's great to be with someone who is representing your concerns and sharing in your ideals. It also increases your feeling of being bonded because your work together is making the world a better place.

If you are with a giving person, consider yourself very lucky and find a way to create an energetic equality with the person who is there for you. Even if you think things are equal, ask your partner what he or she thinks, just in case. It is also wise to remember that acknowledgment and appreciation are important, even if never asked for.

No matter how giving a person may be, no one can live by giving alone. I can't imagine Mother Teresa getting a pedicure, but I'm sure she had a way of recharging. We all need to rest and take in energy to survive.

Here are some tips to help you and your partner give your best.

♡ *People usually give to others in the way they would like to be given to, so figuring out how to give back to your partner should be easy. Pay attention to what your partner does for you and how he or she does it, and then give back in return. The other easy way to find out what your partner might need is to simply ask. Talk for ten minutes about how to create more of what each of you wants and needs from the other. The object is for both of you to feel good about what you give and are given.*

♡ *Ask your partner to make a list of things that he or she would like to receive from you but that are not material items. Make your own list for your partner. You may include spending a day with you at the beach, serving you breakfast in bed, or going with you to visit a friend or relative. If you're a fisherman, you might really like to have your mate go fishing with you one day. True, you may have to bait the hook, but you'll laugh until your sides ache when your partner lands a first catch. A woman who is active in her community may love it if the man in her life attends high tea with her and the other ladies in the group. These nonmaterial ways of giving create intimacy in a way that lasts. Knowing that your partner is willing to give the most valuable thing of all, his or her time, is truly heartwarming.*

Now Honey, Pick Up Your Mess

Savers can find balance with spenders (see chapter 31 for some helpful tips). Early birds and night owls can achieve true harmony. Even Energizer bunnies and cat people can meet in the middle. (If you and your love are any of these, see chapters 21 and 22.) And it turns out, even a neat freak and an untidy person can find true happiness.

Messiness is a common issue among couples. Most of the time, one partner wants the other to be less messy. Responding to this concern may be just a matter of creating a new behavior or two. For many, leaving dirty socks on the floor or wet towels in a pile is simply a bad habit that may have been created during childhood. If you've always had someone picking up after you, how would you have learned to pick up after yourself?

For others, such habits stem from laziness, which is a reflection of an overall attitude toward life. This is a problem that, if not addressed, can lead to bigger problems in your relationship. There is a difference between living a relaxed, low-stress life and living a lazy one. The first helps to keep you healthy as you move toward your goals, while the second gives you carpal tunnel syndrome from clicking the remote control.

For a few people, messiness is a passive-aggressive means of getting attention or giving payback, which seldom works and always causes more problems than it's worth. It's a sign of a deeper issue, and this is where consulting with a marriage counselor may be an appropriate option.

In most cases, couples can solve messiness dilemmas on their own. If you want the house to be tidier, the first thing you have to do is identify that messiness is a problem for you. This means that you have to talk about it, which may be the most difficult part. The goal is to come to an agreement as to how you can live together and maintain a level of clean and neat that works for both of you.

If your time is too valuable to spend cleaning bathrooms, you need to be willing to hire a housekeeper rather than put the entire burden on your partner. It will also make the one you love feel cared for.

If you tend to be the less tidy partner, and your partner wants more order, bear in mind that keeping the house neater is an act of love. Being neater may also benefit you personally. Order can help us find balance in our lives and provide an emotional safety net. When life throws you a curve, keeping your life and home organized will assist you in maintaining peace of mind. Look at this task as a compromise, not a condemnation.

If you are the neat freak, and your partner still doesn't get what you're asking, you might want to step back and reconsider whether it's so important. Concentrate on all your partner's wonderful qualities and ask yourself if your desire for order is worth the stress of continuing to ask your partner to change. Perhaps you may be best served by putting aside your frustration. Seen this way, picking up after your partner is also an act of love.

These simple tips can help you put the bliss back into your life and keep clutter from pushing you away from the one you love.

♡ *Ask your partner to take ten minutes with you to straighten the house. Pick a time you both find comfortable (perhaps after dinner). This ritual can actually increase your intimacy by making the person who requires neatness feel cared for. If you're the messy one, think of it as a gift you are giving to make your love's life nicer.*

♡ *If you just can't be neat enough for your partner, and he or she is willing to pick up after you, try doing a tradeoff and wash the car or take on some other task to help create balance.*

♡ *There is a difference between clean and neat. Your partner may do his or her part in keeping the house clean, but it's* still messier than you'd like. Try using hampers for dirty clothes and towels, hooks for hanging things, and containers for magazines and newspapers. With as little as ten minutes of discussion and a quick trip to a bed and bath store, you may find that you're closer to a compromise than you thought.

Look for What's Right

It's very easy to find flaws in your relationship or with your partner if you're looking for them. Some people make it a hobby and then wonder why things don't feel good anymore.

Many couples are caught up in what I call a negative feedback loop, where both people are constantly in a defensive mode. In order to break this kind of destructive pattern, you first have to identify it. Then you can do something about it.

If the two of you have been continually sniping at each other, I suggest that you simply start being nice to your partner. It may sound a little trite, but when you've only been getting negativity, a little niceness goes a long way toward helping you both change course. Try it for a week and I believe that you will see a significant difference in your relationship and with your attitude toward life. Getting acknowledgment from the one you love can turn a dark day into a bright one.

If both people in the relationship realize they are equally responsible for the difficulties, it's actually empowering because it gives you the ability to change the dynamic of how you relate. But again, don't wait for your partner to make the first move toward changing things for the better. You can begin to deal with the problem by finding a way to give a little extra kindness to the person you're committed to.

This method is simple, but the trick is to make it consistent. Knowing that your partner is there with you and you're working through the process together will make it easier for both of you to see that the glass is not only half full; it's overflowing.

It also helps to realize that you actually have a good relationship, even though things may not be rosy at the moment. There are many reasons why the two of you fell in love and decided to engage in the relationship dance. Remembering those reasons and looking for that familiar light in your loved one's eyes will help inspire you to take the steps you need to get things back on track.

Life is about transitioning through problems as gracefully as possible. Having relationship issues doesn't mean that either one of you is a failure; it means that you're human. Trusting that you are meant to be together and you want to stay that way will help you rise to the occasion. Once you learn to accentuate the positive, your relationship will become inspirational.

Instead of going on a Columbo-like investigation looking for problems, you may want to emphasize the great things that your partner does. Here are some tips.

♡ Create a list of three positive things your partner does and one area where you'd like your partner to improve. Ask your partner to do the same thing. After you complete your lists, read them to each other. Begin with the positives. Both of you should really soak up what's said. After this, it will be much easier for each of you to take in the area that needs improvement. The three-to-one ratio lets each partner really focus on healing rather than just feeling bad. Having to deal with more than one emotional issue or change at a time can be too taxing. Give yourselves a day to think about it, ask questions for clarity if you need to, and start bringing solutions to the table that night over dinner. Each of you should keep your focus on your partner's concern. Also, keep the conversations short, ten minutes max.

♡ Spend the next week catching your partner doing something right and thanking her or him when you see it. If your partner does this with you, the two of you may want to celebrate at the end of the week by going out to dinner, opening a bottle of wine, or just giving each other a big kiss. Again, this reinforces the desire and ability to make changes in other areas. And you can make it a daily routine if you like. Couples who make it a routine have happier and more intimate relationships because they feel emotionally supported.

Ten Tips for Compromising

*S*omewhere in a thesaurus far, far away, there is another word for marriage—and it is "compromise." Each letter in this word, which has somehow gotten left out of the wedding vows, gives couples direction in how to take a relationship from the battlefield to blissful coexistence.

> *C*—Compromise is something that combines qualities or elements of different things. It does not mean giving up or giving in. It is a blending of hearts and minds, and that is what makes a marriage. So learn to compromise.

> *O*—Open your whole heart. Even holding back as little as 1 percent can make the difference between a loving and a losing relationship.

M—Maximize your willingness. Just being willing to bend a little will encourage new ways of relating. The space you create allows you to change in ways you never imagined. Anyone who has ever grown in a relationship will tell you how much better the relationship has become over time.

P—Promise is the second half of compromise. It means to communicate your commitment and dedication to the one you love. Do this on a daily basis, and you will have a long-lasting and loving relationship.

R—Release your desire for control. Giving up having to be right or getting your way will make your life much easier. In addition, you are actually giving a gift to yourself (and your partner) by releasing any pent-up anger or fear. By holding on to the need to control, you are actually being controlled by your unhealthy emotions.

O—Optimistic couples have longer and healthier lives and relationships than those who are pessimistic. Do your best to look on the bright side, and know that the dark times are almost always temporary. This attitude will make dealing with any situation easier.

M—Minimize your defensiveness. When your partner tells you something that you may need to hear, try to listen and consider what he or she has to say before you react. One of the best parts of being in a relationship is having someone there to help you look and be your best.

I—Inspiration is one of the greatest gifts a relationship can offer. Being connected can make you want to be creative and grow in ways you may never have thought of if you were alone. Let your relationship inspire you to do great things.

S—Selflessness gets you more than you could ever want. Give what you want to receive, and you will communicate to your partner what it is you desire. You may also find that by giving to your partner, you will see your needs diminish as the love between you grows.

E—Engage with your mate. Rather than trying to ignore or disconnect with the person you love, take a giant step toward him or her. It makes the experience of being in a relationship, as well as your communication, whole.

Compromise is not a hard lesson once you realize the gifts that come from it. Learning to work with your partner will make your relationship and your life a better place to be.

PART
5

Intimate

Challenges

Chapter 28

Bad Days

*E*veryone has bad days. They can come from feeling physically unwell, being stressed or emotionally drained, and many other reasons. When your partner is the one having the bad day, you may notice that it's contagious and you feel bad as well. This is a situation that can be remedied (and it needs to be) with a little understanding and a few simple techniques.

First, realize that someone else's mood is not your responsibility, even if your partner tells you it is (unless you have intentionally hurt him or her). The truth is that we all have bad days occasionally and we all deal with them differently.

If you are the type of person who tries everything you can to pull your partner out of his or her bad days, your loved one is lucky to have you. However, despite your best efforts, you may not be able to change how your partner feels. On those occasions, you need to understand that he or she is in the process of healing, which may require some internal work. That may mean curling up on the couch with a cup of chicken soup and the television, while others may need to go to bed and pull the covers up over their heads.

If that process makes you feel shut out or powerless, that's understandable, but realize that sometimes you can't help your partner feel better. If your partner is not being open to your suggestions or your overtures of kindness, or doesn't respond to your best jokes, don't take it personally. There are times when the only thing you can do for the one you love is to just be there.

This doesn't mean that you give your partner the silent treatment and cop an attitude yourself. Doing so will only pour salt on the wound. The trick here is to maintain your normal demeanor and be available when your partner is ready to talk. Understanding that everyone needs a little inner processing time every now and then will help you to deal with this occasional departure from your normal routine.

If you are the one who is having a bad day, avoid inflicting your discomfort on your partner. Simply let him or her know that you need a little quiet time right now. If you reassure your mate that you love him or her, your partner will be less likely to take what you're going through personally.

If you or your loved one withdraws on a regular basis, it is a sign that there may be other issues, such as depression. If you believe that something more serious may exist, do whatever you can to get yourself or your partner a thorough medical and psychological evaluation as soon as possible. If your partner is reluctant to move forward on this, you will need to insist on it.

Having a bad day is a part of life. Knowing how to get through it in a manner that won't foster disharmony will provide both of you with many more days to create beautiful music together.

Here's a tip for how you and your partner can help each other get through those bad days.

♡ *When you are both feeling upbeat (and your partner is willing to work on this problem), have a discussion about what each of you would like from the other when you feel down. Write down the top three things you'd like each other to do the next time it happens, and keep the lists where you both can find them. Here are some helpful activities to explore: Do you prefer to be left alone to go on the computer? Would he like you just to snuggle beside him on the couch while you both watch a brainless TV show? Does she just want you to ask her how she's feeling and then commiserate with her as she vents?*

Making Peace with Your Partner's Past

$\mathcal{T}$here may be a thing or two in your loved one's past that you are still having trouble dealing with. Perhaps your partner sowed a few too many wild oats, or as Bette Midler put it, "was way into double digits" when describing his or her quantity of ex-lovers. Perhaps your partner lived in a different way than the two of you do now or once ran with a rough crowd.

Whatever the circumstances, you need to find a way to put past behaviors where they belong: in the past. If every time you look into your mate's eyes and you see her or him doing things that make you uneasy, it's going to be difficult for you to fully attach. It can also cause you to withdraw or get angry when "old friends" of your beloved are around.

In order to deal with this discomfort, you have to slow down, take a deep breath, and really see where the problem lies. If your mate has grown up and changed, and is a good partner, then the problem may not belong to him or her. Unfortunately, the burden of letting go falls on you.

We all have baggage. The trick is not to let it take up space in your current relationship. I know it's easier said than done, but letting go of the past is going to help you relish the moment. It will also deepen your relationship.

Stuffing your feelings isn't going to help; denial never gets you where you hope it will. Your best bet in this situation is to confront the demon head-on and let yourself (and your partner) know that you're not going to let ghosts of the past ruin your present.

Having this conversation is a big leap toward resolution because talking about the things that bother us with our loved ones is the most powerful healing tool we have. Putting your feelings on the table will make both of you feel lighter.

Acceptance may be your best mechanism for dealing with these kinds of issues. If you love and respect your mate, and you like the way your partner treats you and those close to you, go this route. Try accepting that who your partner was in the past has helped your partner become the person he or she is today. Doing so will help you resolve many unhealed issues in this arena.

Making peace with your partner's past will empower both of you to appreciate your relationship and fully enjoy each other, now and in the future.

Here are some tips to help you make peace with the past.

♡ Have a conversation with your partner about it. If there's something about your partner's past that bothers you, talk about it. Ask if there's anything about your past that bothers your partner. Agree to let it all go and do a simple ritual to let go of the past: throw a reminder of troubling times or actions of the past into the fireplace and watch it burn together.

♡ If a painful memory involves a location that is within driving distance, make a date to visit that place. It could be the old family home, a cemetery, or even a school. Your job is to just be there for your partner while she or he grieves, cries, or just releases pent-up feelings about the issues. There may not be a need to say anything. Being present for someone who is confronting the pain of their past is a loving gesture that can't help but deepen your relationship.

♡ Make a pact with your partner that neither of you will bring up former (real or perceived) shortcomings in each other the next time you have a disagreement.

Chapter 30

Job Stress and Relationships

$\mathcal{T}$he workday is over and you're looking forward to having a lovely evening with your mate. Upon arriving home, you find your partner staring blankly into the computer screen with a pained look on her face. "What's wrong?" you ask with empathy. Your partner responds, "My department is getting reorganized and I'm worried about my job."

When you're ready to play and your partner is stressed out, how can the two of you join forces and find a way to enjoy your time together? First of all, you need to realize that your partner isn't doing anything inappropriate but is just reacting to a perceived threat. Some people can blow these things off while others will let insecurity take over.

Your job as a loving partner is to be the voice of reason and to comfort your mate by pointing out that it's normal to feel a little stress under the circumstances. It's also helpful to be reassuring and remind the one you love that you will always be there. Statements like "It's okay, because if anything happens, we'll get through this together" can help ease the anxiety and increase your closeness.

Emotionally pumping up your partner is one of the most important parts of a thriving relationship. By the time your partner returns to work and calls to say that everything is fine, while thanking you for your unrelenting support, your relationship will have grown stronger.

It's a blessing to know that if you're ever feeling down, the one you love will be there to help lift you back up. Knowing you can count on your mate when things are shaky is a gift that only an intimate relationship can give you.

Here are some tips for easing work-related stress or fear of job loss.

♡ *First, understand that your partner may need a little time to calm down. Taking a couple of hours to relax can reduce the tension of stressful thoughts. Sometimes a person needs to "sleep on it" in order to gain a proper perspective. Many situations can look a lot brighter in the fresh light of day.*

♡ *If your partner is still stressed out the next morning, there are several things you can do to help encourage him or her out of the doldrums. Taking a walk together is a great stress reliever. You might also consider taking the day off.*

♡ *If your partner is concerned about possibly losing a job, one thing you can do to help is to emphasize how good your partner is at what he or she does for a living. Remind the one you love of past achievements. Talking about your partner's other skills and options can also ease this stressful time.*

♡ *Many couples create contingency plans when things are going well to help ease the stress of life's inevitable curveballs. Brainstorm with your partner about what you would do if one of you lost your job. You may discuss starting your own business, early retirement, going back to school, or even changing careers or cities.*

Love and Money

$\mathcal{S}$ome people feel better when they have a little extra money in their pockets while others feel it instantly burning a hole in their wallet. Somehow or other, spenders and savers seem to find each other in otherwise blissful relationships. Perhaps opposites do attract, but in this area, you can make the attraction last much longer if you can get on the same page with your partner sooner rather than later. It's well documented that money is one of the main reasons for relationship discord and breakups, even among the most civilized of couples. It is actually the reason for 30 percent of all divorces.

If you're afraid to bring up your financial fears or tell your partner your real feelings about his or her spending habits, get over it! This dangerous ostrich approach will come back to bite you. Get your head out of the sand and look at (and talk about) what's going on in the money department.

Buying a home in an uncertain market, planning for retirement, and trying to make ends meet are just some of the issues that contemporary couples must face. With the cost of living skyrocketing, everyone is feeling a little more anxious about money these days. And that kind of thinking has a neutralizing effect on intimacy. In order to make the financial side of life go as easy as possible, you and your partner both have to get comfortable talking about this uncomfortable topic.

If you wait too long to bring up the topic of money, just getting started can create uncomfortable feelings. At that point, you simply have to ignore your discomfort and dive right in. Fortunately, there are a number of places you can go for help before you and your partner wind up throwing your checkbooks at each other.

Try using a workbook like *The Couple's Guide to Love and Money* by Jonathan Rich (2003). Tools like these can be highly beneficial, especially when you just don't know where to begin. Rich believes that couples can work out their money matters by understanding how differing "financial personalities" affect the relationship, and helps them work through conflicts about anything from spending to building wealth.

If you are a saver, the anxiety created by constant debt can cause you to withdraw emotionally. If you are a spender, your spending habits may be creating stress for your partner and for your relationship. It is also possible that the stress of the relationship is causing you to spend money in a compulsive way in order to make yourself feel better, and it's become a destructive pattern.

Another way that you and your partner can deal with your current financial differences is to examine how each of you grew up. How our families dealt with money has a lot to do with our financial styles. You may want to consult other books or websites on financial matters. There are even counselors who specialize in financial issues for couples, but be careful and make sure the person you go to for help is licensed and experienced.

If you think that bringing up the business side of your relationship isn't romantic, you're right, but it is necessary for your relationship's survival. Trust me, thinking about how you're going to pay the bills is a real romance killer. It's amazing how much easier it is to be intimate once you get your financial house in order by coming to agreements, taking care of issues, and not letting things slide.

Merging your financial expectations may seem daunting at first, but think of the repercussions if you don't. The truth is that you and your partner probably want the same things and just have differing ways of approaching those goals. Talking about your dreams may be a good topic, because once the two of you agree on where you want to end up, getting on the same path is a lot easier.

So circumvent the difficulties that not having an appropriate understanding about your finances will cause, and sit down with your partner and your accountant. The end result will be one that your relationship will profit from.

Here are some tips to help you and your partner get the money stuff ironed out.

♡ *Many couples don't talk about money at all. But in order to create a secure financial future, you have to be willing to discuss what does and doesn't work for you. Sit down with* your partner this evening and start the discussion. You don't need a game plan at this point; the idea is to agree that you need to create one.

♡ To get the real process started, get your checkbooks, bills, and spreadsheets on the table, literally. Put them all on the main table in your house. They don't have to be organized. Just seeing all that paperwork will force the two of you to talk about paying your bills, creating a budget, and looking at your spending habits. You can make putting your papers in order your first task after you agree to start talking. Leave the piles where they are for motivation. They are a strong visual reminder that you have work to do, and it's important to the well-being of your relationship to make sure you don't ignore it any longer.

♡ Once you and your partner come up with a budget, set aside some amount as disposable income. It doesn't have to be large, but it gives the spender the ability to indulge that need while also not going overboard and stressing out the saver.

♡ If you and your partner find that you just can't make sense out of your finances, or you continue to butt heads, go see a financial counselor. Just make sure the counselor is a certified financial planner (has a CFP license) and get a recommendation from someone you trust.

Get Closer

A relationship done right is an intimate experience. That being said, with intensely busy schedules, many couples wake up one day to find that the person they are looking at across the breakfast table has become a stranger. When this happens, the journey back to the land of closeness isn't quite as complicated as finding your way around a foreign country, but it does require trying new ways to connect. First, you need to take the risk of asking your partner to come a little closer. It's worth the effort and can help direct the two of you to a place where you can reunite and enjoy the rest of your life's journey.

Sit down with your partner and talk about all the wonderful things that he or she has done for you over the years. What were they? How have you reciprocated? These questions will help the two of you rediscover the love between you without creating an atmosphere of discomfort. Just looking at the good stuff for a little while can shine a new light on your romance, and things can quickly turn around.

Seeing disconnects as misunderstandings can also keep your relationship where you want it to be. When you have your partner's best interest at heart, and you believe that she or he feels the same way, you need to accept that even if your feelings get hurt, it isn't coming from a mean place.

The key to finding your way back to each other is to trust that you are loved. If you're wondering why your partner is still with you, I suggest that you ask why, not in a challenging way, but as a means of rediscovering one another. Asking "Honey, why are you with me?" will create a very powerful moment. Yes, there may be a few awkward seconds, but once you start the conversation, you will find that you are together for many more reasons than you may have thought.

Getting close again is a choice that, if you both make it together, will become a self-fulfilling desire. Intimacy comes from and speaks to the heart, but you must be open to receive it. Check out your emotions and see if there's something blocking you from being close. Chances are, if there is, it's old stuff that you could let go. Then you'll have room for some tenderness and some fun.

If you and your partner have drifted to different parts of the sea, don't wait for your partner to grab an oar. Take the initiative, and soon you will both be paddling your way back to each other. The relief you feel once you are truly back in each other's arms is a real lifesaver.

Reconnecting with your partner is easier when you remember why it is you love each other. With modern life being so complicated, it's possible to forget that part. Try these exercises to get you started.

♡ *As soon as you feel that you are out of touch with your partner, do something to reconnect. Your dilemma is not as complicated or scary as it may seem. All that is required is a desire on both your parts to make your relationship a little bit closer. Make a regular date night or take a weekend away. And make a pact with your partner to have a little fun every day.*

♡ *Here's a wonderful exercise for you and your partner. Hold hands and look into each other's eyes and remember why you fell in love in the first place. Why is this person so special to you? How was your partner able to capture your heart and hold it? Talk about these things with each other. This alone will help to make your relationship whole again.*

Ten Tips for Getting Your Needs Met

*M*any people don't know how to ask for what they need in their relationship. The trick is to talk about your own feelings. Here are ten nonconfrontational methods that will help you get your emotional desires met.

1. *If you want your partner to improve, get good at making observations.*

   Watch how your partner behaves and be prepared to point out that behavior to your mate in a loving and constructive manner. Blasting someone is not empathetic; it's unkind.

2. *Discuss the real behaviors that are affecting your relationship.*

   These need to be delivered without opinions. Discuss what specific behaviors you see that you don't feel good about. (Example: "The other day when I was talking, you interrupted me.")

3. *Look at how you are feeling. Are you angry?*

   Do you feel cheated or let down? If so, you need to tell your partner without belittling him or her. If you present your feelings honestly, a person who loves you will naturally do his or her best to make things right.

4. *Be clear about what you need.*

   Do you want change, understanding, or compatibility? Whatever your need is, asking for it directly will greatly improve your chances of getting it. If your partner doesn't know what you need, or if you expect him or her to read your mind, nothing will change.

5. *Make a single request.*

   By asking your partner for one specific change, you greatly increase the probability of getting your needs met. It's best to state your request in gentle terms, like "In the future, would you be willing to..."

6. *Actively address the issue or let it go.*
   Stockpiling (continuing to bring up old topics) will not help to heal your issue. State your needs, have a discussion, and reach a resolution so that you can move on, or agree with your partner that you will readdress the problem at another time in the near future.

7. *Become more realistic in your expectations.*
   Making your expectations realistic is not the same as lowering them, and you can still have your dreams. It's healthier to have preferences rather than expectations, so you won't feel as disappointed if your preference isn't met.

8. *Tell your partner what you want, not what you don't want.*
   Be honest and be kind. Letting your partner know exactly what you want, and keeping it positive, will make his or her job much easier.

9. *Truly value the contribution your partner has made to your life.*
   When people feel valued, they tend to do the best they can to keep your opinion of them high. Remind your mate that you know your life is better because your mate is in it. Doing so can be very motivational and loving.

10. *Balance is key to maintaining an emotionally fit and close relationship.*

Do your best to reserve the time and energy you need to devote to your intimacy and to your partner.

Getting your needs met requires that you remain aware of your own emotional needs as well as those of the one you love.

PART
6

Intimate

Repair

How to Deepen Mutual Respect

There is a component of relationships that is just as important as love, trust, and communication—respect. When this quality is missing or when respect is not mutual, it can shut the door to joy, peace, and even intimacy.

Showing respect for your partner is as simple as calling when you think you may be late from work. It also shows up in how you talk to and about the one you love. Keeping it positive will keep your relationship from going negative.

A respectful person will never embarrass you in public or have an argument in front of others. Respecting your love means respecting yourself as well. Couples who share a mutual respect seem to stand a little taller in the eyes of those who know them.

Partners who respect each other raise respectful children and have respectful friends. It's a case of like attracting like. Couples who are respectful lower their stress levels and are more able to work as a true team. This makes solving even the most complicated problems much easier.

Most people can tell when someone doesn't respect them, and receiving that kind of vibe from your mate cuts deeply. Even if you never use your words as weapons, your feelings will be obvious to the one you love. If either of you is disrespectful, you need to put this issue on the table ASAP.

Occasionally acting disrespectfully doesn't mean you are a disrespectful person or that you disrespect your partner. Everyone makes mistakes now and then. The trick is to catch yourself (or let your partner know) right after a disrespectful incident happens.

Sometimes you may feel disrespected even when a behavior isn't objectively disrespectful. If you think you may be overly sensitive and tend to overreact, you can do something about it. Ask yourself if a behavior really is disrespectful, or if it is just triggering something in you.

Sharing your real feelings is your best tool in helping your partner see how his or her behavior may be undermining your relationship. Rebuilding your connection to a mutually respectful relationship may take some time and work, but it's much easier than living in conflict.

Feeling the respect of the one you love and returning it is enlivening and inspirational. Find the love between you and your partner, and use it to take the necessary steps to make things right. It will only add to your intimacy.

Here are some tips to begin to correct the course of your relationship.

♡ *Show your respect for your partner by supporting his or her views when they are different from your own. Your partner may take a political stand that doesn't jibe with yours. Instead of shaking your head in disbelief, simply say to your partner that you respect his or her opinion.*

♡ *If your partner wins an award, whether it be employee of the month or humanitarian of the year, throw a party. It doesn't have to be a big affair. Having a few friends and family gathering at your behest will make your partner feel as proud as having won an Oscar, especially when you make a little speech about how great he or she is.*

♡ *Honor your partner's contribution to the relationship. To formalize your appreciation, sign a photograph with "all my love," and put it in a nice frame. A little thing, perhaps, but it is a constant reminder of your respect.*

Tears Build Intimacy

Studies show that people who repress their feelings fall prey to everything from financial ruin to cancer. The thing you have to remember is that your feelings are there for a reason, and just as your body needs to breathe to stay alive, you need to express your emotions if you want to keep your intimacy strong.

Your pain, if not let out appropriately, can appear as anger or even rage. If held in, it may become depression or apathy. In theory, expressing your emotions is as simple as saying "ouch" when your toe gets stepped on. If you are dealing with an emotionally painful issue, simply state what it is you are feeling. Holding in your emotions isn't a sign of strength; it really says that you're afraid your partner might see how vulnerable you are.

Crying is one of the healthiest things you can do for your emotional self and for your relationship. Some people are afraid to cry because they think that once they start, they may never stop. Indeed, it can seem that way. But in truth, most people are able to work through their emotional issues quicker than they think they will.

Talking about your feelings is also healing. As a couple, you can use two-way communication to help each other get deeper into your hearts and feelings. Talk with your partner until you process your feelings, either by emoting or by just identifying the source of the pain. Afterward, you will feel a sense of relief and you will also feel closer to your partner. The important thing to remember here is that the heart can only hold so much, and if it's full of pain, there's no room for positive emotions.

It's a mistake to think that you can run from your own feelings. No matter how much exercise you get, or how clean you keep your garage or kitchen, you still have to feel whatever is going on inside you. Trying to push down or avoid your emotions is a recipe for future problems—certainly emotional and possibly physical.

So do what you need to do in order to get rid of the pain you feel inside. Nobody will fault you, because we all have felt it and we all will feel it again sooner or later.

Here are some tips to help you let the pain out without straining your intimacy.

♡ *If you need help or a shoulder to cry on, start by asking your partner if he or she would be willing to be there for you while you "have a good cry." As you release your emotional pain, the space in your heart that the pain was taking up will be filled by the love from your partner.*

♡ *Sometimes inner pain can make it difficult to talk. If you have this problem, try writing to your partner about the pain in your heart. This will help you release the pain, understand your own process, and deepen your relationship. Once your partner knows how you are hurting, he or she will have a better understanding of the dynamics in your relationship, and both of you will have shared something deep and meaningful. This will strengthen your connection to one another. After your partner has read your words, you may be much more available to talk about it, release a bit more, and get back to an open and loving place.*

Politeness Fosters Love

*D*o you say "please" when you want something and "thank you" when you get what you've asked for? These simple words can make the difference between a relationship that's thriving and one that's just surviving. When we stop being polite to one another, it is as if a wall begins to grow between us, blocking our intimacy.

Remember how careful you were with each other when you began your courtship? Being polite was part of the charm that helped you decide to spend the rest of your lives together. It's such a simple thing, yet so easily forgotten.

Couples who say they have great relationships point out that simple politeness is one of the reasons for their success. The act of asking your partner if he or she would like anything when you go into the kitchen is an example of the kind of behavior I'm suggesting. It makes relationships flourish because it says to your partner, "I care about you."

It's all about finding those places where you can give your partner a little gift of the heart. These random acts of kindness have a powerful effect on your relationship. If you have any doubt, try it. You'll find that any action to show you care will be rewarded and returned.

Here are some tips to help you raise the politeness quotient in your relationship.

♡ *If you've let your politeness fade, it's never too late to recover it. Simply say "thank you" the next time your partner does something for you. Not overlooking the little things makes a big difference in a relationship.*

♡ *If you feel that it's your partner who has forgotten how to be nice, see if he or she picks up on it after you first set the example. If not, you may want to explain that it's a way that he or she can express love for you.*

♡ *If you are a man, show the woman you love how much you care by opening doors for her and pulling out her chair at a restaurant. These gallant actions will remind her that she truly has found her knight in shining armor, no matter how badly it may have been tarnished in the past.*

♡ *If you are a woman, express your gratitude when the man in your life takes the extra step to show he cares. This is the appropriate response to any noble gesture. If you want to return the favor, politeness to a man can mean asking if he'd like a coffee refill or a snack.*

Receiving Love Is as Important as Giving It

$\mathcal{I}$t may be more blessed to give than to receive, but many people have a hard time accepting gifts, compliments, and even love. This can make for a lonely life and a pervasive sense of not being good enough.

If you find that you have trouble truly receiving your partner's gifts, compliments, or other signs of love for you, your inability to feel deserving may block many of the good things in life. Allowing yourself to accept these things can be a difficult task, but it's worth the effort.

You may be preventing your partner from giving to you by the way you react when receiving a gift. If you pull away from your partner when she or he reaches for you, but you also feel unloved, then you may need to examine your own reaction to receiving affection.

Notice how you feel when your partner pays you a compliment or gives you a gift. Often people who have difficulty receiving love feel guilty or unworthy when someone does something nice for them.

Ask yourself if you feel you deserve the love you are getting, and if the love you are getting is the kind of love you want. If you find that you are unable or unwilling to accept the love that is being offered to you, it may be a sign of a deep resentment that needs to be discussed and worked out. Take your time when examining these questions; they often tend to reflect buried issues such as low self-esteem.

Allowing yourself to receive isn't about what you're getting but about being aware enough to value the gifts life gives you. It's not about material objects or money. It's about realizing that life is a series of gifts that come to each of us in different ways. Sometimes it's fame and fortune, and other times it's the joy of a loving family.

For many people, having the ability to give to others is the greatest gift. They feel love by seeing the glow in the eyes of those they care for and sometimes in the eyes of those they will never know. To be able to contribute to others in this manner is also a way of giving to yourself. If that is who you are, the world is a better place for having you in it.

If you find it difficult to receive your partner's love, try these exercises.

♡ *Listen to the next compliment that your partner gives you. Don't judge it, feel guilty for it, or ignore it. Just say thank you and absorb the good feeling inside you.*

♡ *Have your partner tell you what he likes about you. Listen without commenting on or dismissing or deflecting these statements, either verbally or physically (no rolling your eyes or deep sighs!). Then see how much you can remember of what was said, and share how the experience makes you feel. Next, do the same for your partner. Then ask yourselves, is it easier to give or to receive compliments? By discussing this with your partner, you may well discover that you have some commonalities in this area, and you can help each other get better at receiving kind words.*

♡ *This year, take the time to write a thank-you note to your lover every time he or she gives you a gift, no matter how small. Be sure to express your feelings of gratitude for having him or her in your life, and as you are writing, allow yourself to feel deserving of admiration.*

Ten Tips for Giving Emotional Support

*E*motional support comes in a variety of shapes and sizes. Having the desire and ability to give emotional support to your partner is far more important than doing it exactly right. Here are some tips to help you nourish your sweetheart's heart.

1. *Touch your partner often.*
   Most people are touch starved. Holding hands, walking arm in arm, and cuddling on the couch are just some of the simple ways to share this very powerful experience.

2. Be respectful of your partner's feelings.

If the one you love is dealing with a loss or a disappointment, let him or her know that you are available to talk. Letting your partner have the space to process feelings is another way of showing that you care.

3. Give small gifts just because.

Being surprised every once in a while helps to keep the romance alive and lets your mate know you think he or she is something special.

4. Compliment your partner in front of other people.

Saying nice things about your mate in the presence of friends or associates is one of the most supportive things you can do. Not only will it make your partner feel good; it will make him or her feel great about you.

5. Disagree with your partner in a kind and loving way.

Never judge or reject your mate's ideas or desires without first considering them. If you have a difference of opinion, that's fine, as long as you express it with kindness.

6. Say "I love you."

Actually hearing it is important to many people. You may show your love in many other ways, but actually saying the three little words will reassure your partner.

7. Never ignore your loved one's presence.

There is nothing more hurtful than being treated like you don't exist. Being angry at the moment is no reason to be rude to the person who loves you. Stop and think what life would be like if your sweetheart weren't with you.

8. Listen deeply and take in what your partner is saying.

Your partner will feel nurtured knowing that he or she is being heard. Listening deeply is also the best way to heal old wounds and prevent misunderstandings. Paraphrasing what your partner has said is a great way to let him or her know you are tuned in.

9. Speak in a loving tone and remember to smile.

Your tone of voice and your facial expressions say as much as, if not more than, the words you use. Speaking in a sincere and loving tone will let your loved one know you are coming from a caring place.

10. *If your partner is having a rough time, pull out all the stops.*

Do everything you can to help with or minimize your mate's troubles. It's a true gift to have the person you love by your side when things are rocky.

Emotional support is about helping to lift someone to higher ground, so he or she can see a way through the difficulty. Having someone to rely on when the chips are down is one of the best parts of being in a relationship.

PART
7

Intimate

Living

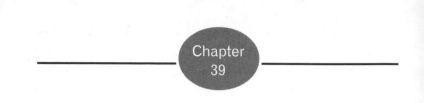
Relationships Are About Running Errands

*A*lmost daily I hear someone tell me about their ideal mate. The description goes something like this: "I want someone to travel with, who will play the sports I like, someone who will take me to nice places."

Although these are all wonderful things, they are also very temporary, and not exactly the qualities that you want to look for in a life mate. But most of our lives are not spent touring Paris, hitting holes in one, or lunching at Spago. Sure it sounds wonderfully romantic, but the truth is that we spend most of our time taking care of home, hearth, and work. Not to mention the kids, animals, and whatever else we have attached ourselves to.

Sure, we'd all like to travel the world and enjoy our free moments on the golf course or walking along the beach. But in reality, we spend much of our time as a couple running errands. I believe that we need to be with someone who makes our daily chores at least tolerable, if not downright pleasant.

Our fantasy lovers would never consider going to the market on a Saturday evening, spending a couple of weekends organizing the garage, or clipping coupons from the Sunday paper. And I doubt that this is something Brad and Angelina have ever done.

Since most of us aren't movie stars, however, we need to put our expectations into perspective. We also need to realize that it's a gift to have a loving companion who helps us endure the stresses of life with as little damage as possible.

Look at your partner again and think to yourself, "Wow, this person has really made the drudgery of daily living much easier." And then, remember to say this to him or her, for your loved one can never hear it enough.

Then thank your lucky stars that you've found someone who isn't going to demand that you fly them to the moon to make them happy. Our days go by so quickly. Don't taint them by not appreciating the love you are fortunate enough to have.

I know that chasing down the blue-light special is far less enticing than relaxing on an exotic island, but in the end, most of our time is spent doing the little things. And doing them is so much easier when you have a sweetheart holding your hand as you meander through the aisles of Kmart.

True lovers joyfully share and appreciate intimate moments like these. After all, the most important thing in a good partner is that he or she is someone who will accept you for who you are.

Here are some tips to help you appreciate doing the little things with your partner.

♡ *Suggest that you make and share your meals together, but do it with a little panache. This often overlooked tool can help you deepen your connection. It isn't just food for your body; when two hearts and four hands are involved, it becomes food for your soul. Don't just have dinner by candlelight. Create dinner by candlelight. To make it easier and less dangerous, prepare the foods that need chopping, cleaning, and cutting beforehand, so all you have to do is put them together. Add a few rose petals on the table for atmosphere, a nice bottle of wine, and some music, and you have an evening to remember.*

♡ *Do something for your mate that he or she hates to do. Getting the spider out of the bathtub or making a midnight run so your partner can have milk with the morning coffee really says I love you. Taking on a chore that your partner can't stand is an act of love. If your partner hates mopping the floor but hates a dirty floor even more, you could volunteer to mop it.*

♡ *If your partner is usually the first one out of bed in the morning, surprise her or him by getting up early and helping prepare for the day ahead. Make the coffee and breakfast, feed the animals and the kids—whatever tasks your partner usually does, try* to do one or two of them. Look for opportunities every day to enhance your connection.

♡ Talk with your partner about what each of you likes and doesn't like to do in the errand department, and also discuss ways to make these tasks more tolerable. If you both can't stand running errands, try doing them together to make the burden lighter. You can even sneak in lunch at a nice place and make it a semi-date.

♡ If you want to take this to the next level, hire someone to cook dinner and set a romantic table while you are out running errands together. When you get home, everything will be ready for a surprise romantic evening. And worry about the dishes tomorrow.

Intimacy Is a Process

*A*ppreciating the process of love, not just the big events (weddings, trips, anniversaries), is a sign that your relationship has reached a more mature, intimate level.

Relationships that fire up quickly tend to burn out at the same rate. Everybody loves "hot and heavy," but how many people do you know who have it in the long term? Truth is that if sex is what you base your relationship on, there are going to be problems down the line.

Cultivate the deeper things, especially communication. Couples who plant seeds of trust and connection, who grow together over time, will blossom. Sure, there will be rough moments: times when you want to rip the petals off the flower. Nevertheless, if you hang in there, you may find that getting through the difficult times actually creates greater intimacy and understanding.

Having your mate as a best friend may not sound hot to Paris Hilton, but true friendship is the best way to establish a strong connection. Here are a few pointers for creating a great and long-lasting relationship.

First, avoid comparing your relationship with the couples you read about in *People* magazine. The love lives many public figures lead may seem wildly romantic, but we are all aware of the short-lived marriages, tragic breakups, and devastated families that result from these superficial connections.

Trust yourself and your partner to get through the rough patches. When you're in the middle of an upset, it can be hard to see the right thing to do. This is where intimacy and history can come into play. Couples who have had to deal with some adversity find it easier to believe that they will make it through. When a relationship is newer, that bond hasn't been created, so adversity can cause couples to emotionally split and go to separate corners and sometimes separate lives.

When things get uncomfortable, you can stabilize your relationship by taking your time and not giving up. Doing so will create a strong foundation upon which you can both build a future together.

Hang in there. Most successful couples have stuck it out through some difficult periods. If you hang together through the trials and tribulations of resentment, miscommunication, and differences of opinion, there is a good chance that you will have a long and loving relationship.

Here are some tips to help you with the process.

♡ *Spend a few minutes every day taking in the joy of being in an intimate relationship. Watching your lover sleeping, stroking your partner's face or hand as you breakfast together, or* saying the words "I appreciate you" are all very intimate ways of showing your love.

♡ Talk with your partner about how each of you processed your last upsetting incident. Did either of you hold a grudge? Were both of you able to easily let go or did it take some time? Did things change after you talked? What could you both do differently the next time you have a conflict?

♡ Take some time to show your appreciation for your partner. Most of us are rushing around getting things done, and we forget to show our gratitude for what we have and the person we're with. Upon occasion, I like to brush my partner's hair as a way of showing my love. She appreciates the attention and pampering. In exchange, if I've been very good, I get a foot rub. You can also think outside of the box. Fly your partner's family in for a surprise visit or send your love a card every day for a month.

Do You Validate?

$\mathcal{B}$eing validated means a lot more than getting free parking. The kind of validation I'm referring to means consciously acknowledging the things your partner says or does that make you feel appreciated. Being validated can be as simple as hearing the words "I love you" or as subtle as knowing that your picture is on your love's desk. It's validating to know that your love thinks of you throughout the day.

Relationships in which partners validate each other have less conflict and more intimacy. Validation makes you feel good about yourself and your relationship because it confirms the love between you and your partner. Mutual validation helps both of you feel safe and therefore closer.

When someone feels unvalidated, it diminishes the quality of the relationship and creates barriers to intimacy. A lack of validation takes away the strength a person needs to solve life's problems. It also leads to self-destructive behavior, which will only serve to undermine your connection.

If you're not getting the validation you need, it could be because your partner's parents never modeled this behavior. Growing up in a home where there was no validation teaches you that it isn't a necessary part of life, which is just plain wrong. Talk with your partner about your need for validation. You can say something like "Every now and then, I need you to tell me that you think I'm wonderful or beautiful." Also ask what it is your partner needs to feel validated. Then put what you've learned into action.

If, no matter what is said or done, you can't seem to make your partner feel validated, it may be that he or she is dealing with an inner turmoil. The answer here is to help your partner see his or her emotional pain, so it can be healed. Pointing out in a loving way that there may be some deeper issues going on, and that you're willing to do all you can to be supportive, will open the door to change.

Validation is a skill that, with a little practice, can change a relationship for the better. Start using validating behaviors on a regular basis, and they will soon become a habit. Once you and your partner continually engage in this uplifting practice, your relationship will be on a higher level, and you'll be enjoying the view together.

Learning how to validate your partner is a relatively simple skill to master. Here are some tips for creating more validation in your relationship.

♡ *If your partner is feeling down, let him or her know that it's okay to have a bad day and that you are there to be supportive. On the other hand, if your partner has had a success* like a promotion or a great golf game, make a big deal out of it and go out to celebrate.

♡ Other validating actions include giving compliments, expressing empathy, disagreeing in a respectful way, and paying attention to the one you love. Let your partner know that you truly understand and resonate with her or his experience. This can be very validating.

♡ Write a long list of the things your partner has done that make you feel validated. Include the little things as well as the biggies. This should take up at least two pages. Now read the list out loud to your partner. Ask your partner to do the same thing for you. This exercise will take more than ten minutes to do but is worth it. It's a reminder of all the effort you both have put into the relationship, which can't help but make you feel loved, wanted, and, yes, validated.

Chapter 42

Laughter Is the Best Therapy

*A*fter several years of bills, kids, aging, and the assorted pleasures of life as we know it, couples can actually lose their sense of humor. We are truly blessed if our partner can continue to make us laugh every day.

It's important to remember how to laugh. Knowing when not to take things personally and maintaining a sense of humor about the little things will help you in life and in your relationship.

I've learned a lot about the importance of humor from Dr. Bernie Siegel, the author of *Love, Medicine and Miracles* (Harper, 1990); *Prescriptions for Living* (Harper, 1999); and numerous other books. Bernie's been married for fifty years, and for about the same amount of time, he's been working with the terminally ill. If you think your job is stressful, try dealing with dying people on a daily basis.

In one of our radio interviews, Bernie shared with me that when he gets a little cranky or raises his voice, his wife usually says something like "Dear, you're upsetting the animals" or "You're so handsome." Her humorous responses remind him that he may be taking himself a little too seriously. As a pioneer in the field of working with the terminally ill, he also understands that "laughter is the best medicine" and applies it in his own life as well as his work.

Having a sense of humor in your relationship is not only about laughter; it's about finding the silver lining in anything that even resembles a cloud. It's about being a cheerleader when your partner is down and pulling yourself back up when you go there as well.

It's interesting to note that doctors have known for decades that our brains produce a wonderful chemical called endorphins when we laugh. The endorphins increase our resistance to pain, improve our immune system, and make us physically feel good. So humor is good for the body as well as the soul.

Using humor in your relationship is great. Just remember to avoid making a joke at your partner's expense. Making your partner the butt of your joke or embarrassing him or her in front of others is not only inappropriate; it's downright abusive. Be aware that sarcasm can wound people. It may be amusing to you, but teasing can be hurtful to the person it's aimed at.

If the two of you have been through a dark time recently, finding things that make you both smile may seem challenging at first, so be patient. Remember that you're halfway to success when you become aware that there's something missing from your life and you want to find it again.

When the picture's not so rosy, you can look for some humor in what's going on, even if it's a little dark. Being able to laugh at yourself not only makes your problems seem smaller but opens your heart to your partner who is laughing with you.

None of us gets out of here alive, and you'll enjoy your life and your relationship a lot more by sharing as much joy and laughter with your partner as you can.

Here are some tips for rediscovering the laughter in your relationship.

♡ *If the two of you haven't laughed together in a while, rent some comedies at the video store, or suggest going to a funny movie to get things rolling.*

♡ *If you have kids, ask them to share some of their favorite jokes with you and your partner (kid jokes are almost as funny as watching your kid tell them).*

♡ *Create a special evening with your partner during which you share your own stand-up comedy routines with each other or share the things about your lives that give you a belly laugh. Make it a regular thing to share humorous e-mails, comics, or articles with your partner. This has a lovely bonding effect.*

The One-Night Vacation

$\mathcal{I}$n one of my favorite old Gary Cooper movies, *Friendly Persuasion*, after a minor spat, he and his wife end up spending the night in their barn (and away from the kids). As they stroll back to the house the next morning, he asks, "Can we go back there again sometime?" She just looks at him and smiles as she pulls a piece of straw from his shirt.

One of the most romantic things you can do with your partner is to surprise him or her with a one-night vacation. A one-night vacation is also something you can plan together or take turns planning, if you decide you like it and want to "go back there again sometime."

It doesn't have to cost a small fortune. In fact, if you have a barn (with suitable accoutrements), that could work too, but it may be best to take the more modern route. Find a nearby hotel or B&B, and not just anyplace will do. It should be romantic—the more romantic, the better. It also has to have room service. What I am saying here is that if it remotely resembles a Motel 6, cross it off the list.

Finding the time seems to be the biggest deterrent to getting away. With this one-night plan, the two of you can easily sneak away in the middle of the week, even if you have kids at home. And if you don't have children in the nest, this is still a wonderful way to reclaim the spark and add a little sweetness to your relationship.

Doing things differently, changing it up a little here and there, is not only good for your romance; it builds your bond and makes you look at your partner differently. When one of you goes out of your way to make the relationship more fun, it's an act of love, and it can't help but make your connection a little bit deeper.

For those with busy lives, making this romantic gesture a regular treat is a great way to keep your intimacy alive, as well as give you both something to look forward to on a regular basis.

Here are a few extra tips to help make your one-night vacation the sweetest.

♡ *When you check in, ask if there's a honeymoon suite, and if there is and it isn't occupied, ask if the management would be kind enough to let you have it for the same price as a standard room. What's the worst that could happen? They say no and you still have a nice room. If they do upgrade you, your time may be a little bit more magical.*

♡ *Most nice places know how to stage a room with candles and rose petals on the bed. This is also something you can do yourselves in five minutes. Pack candles and a bottle of champagne, if you like. Just make sure that the place you're staying will have anything else you need (glasses, plates for your pastries, and so on). Whether you're at a hotel or a B&B, you can also ask to have breakfast brought to your room.*

The Gift of Time

*M*ark Twain said, "Love seems the swiftest, but is the slowest of all growths. No man or woman knows what perfect love is until they have been married a quarter of a century." Twain may have experienced the common occurrence of once being very angry at his partner—so angry that he and his partner both must have thought a breakup was inevitable, and yet they stayed together—only to realize that whatever the argument was about had been forgotten over the years.

The gift of time gives us the ability to make up for almost any error, whether it is callous or contrived. This is a form of matrimonial magic that couples often overlook. With time and talk, most all of our normal transgressions can be forgiven and some even forgotten. Yes, there are acts that should not be treated as such—violence being the one that stands out the most—but even infidelity can be a growth step in a marriage.

I have witnessed the latter many times in the past two decades of working with couples.

Most people don't employ the patience necessary to make things better. These days, many people decide to leave before considering all their options and, more important, before taking the time to fully investigate the situation. This means looking at your life as a whole: what it was like before your courtship, what it has been like during your relationship, and what it could look like if you choose to stay with the relationship and heal the wounds or, alternatively, to end it.

If your relationship is in trouble, a good rule of thumb is to give it at least six months of serious focus, from the time you begin really working on fixing things and not just being angry about them, before deciding to move on. Both parties will need to commit to this time frame for it to work. Involving yourselves in the healing process means actively engaging in healing your rifts, reading books, going to therapy, and talking things out during this time frame. Put every emotion on the table. You may find that it only takes you six days of intimately discussing your true feelings to heal what's hurting you. I've seen it happen many times before.

Time is our friend when it comes to getting closer and building bonds. If you cut and run before you resolve, or at least fully understand, your differences, you will very likely repeat the same behaviors and make the same choices and mistakes in your next relationship. The only difference will be that it's with another person.

It's wise to remember not to throw away a relationship, just because you think something better may come along. You may find it inspirational to talk with couples you know who have been together for over a decade. Ask them how they did it and what the pluses and minuses are.

Take your time before making any life-altering decisions. I have had a number of people sit on the therapy couch and tell me that they regret leaving their relationship, when there's no going back. Many relationships don't work out, but don't let impatience be the reason you give up.

Here are some tips for letting time be your friend.

♡ *Remember a time when you were so angry or hurt you almost broke up? Talk with your partner about how you feel about the incident now and how you worked it out. If you didn't resolve it, now's your chance. Just share how you feel and give an apology if needed. Don't wait. Do it now.*

♡ *If you're going through a rough time, don't just pack up and leave. Sit down with your partner to talk it out. In all likelihood, the conversation will strengthen your relationship. Even if you and your partner don't resolve all your differences, you will end up in a place where there is more understanding and less hurt. To my way of thinking, it is well worth the effort.*

♡ *Don't let hurt fester. Issues arise because somewhere along the way someone got hurt. Talk with your partner about the pain and do everything you can to help yourself and your partner.*

♡ *If things aren't working, give it some more time. Changes usually take a while. It usually takes at least three months to get used to big changes, such as new jobs, a new home, or the loss of a loved one. If you can heal in that time frame, it's a good sign you have a strong bond.*

Ten Tips for Tenderness

*W*hen tenderness is removed from a relationship, with it goes a sense of security. Here are ten tips for tenderness that will help you keep it.

T—Tender actions mean being gentle. Resorting to "brutal honesty" can make it impossible for someone who is in a sensitive place to hear what you're saying. Be gentle with the one you love.

E—Emotional communication truly comes from the heart, with no thought of winning or taking control. If you've had a rough time, be patient and constant. Give all you can, and trust that your overtures will be returned.

N—Notice how your mate is feeling. Sometimes we get so caught up in our own mini-dramas that we don't even notice when the person we love is feeling hurt or overwhelmed. A kind word at the right time can make the difference between a good day and a bad one.

D—Develop a code, something that only the two of you share: a secret way of touching, a special word that means "I love you," or a look that says everything. These are the things that make a relationship.

E—Easy does it. Anyone who has ever had a bruise knows it stays tender for a while. If you and your partner have hurt one another, go slowly and be caring as you search for a way to meet in the middle and heal your wounds.

R—Respond with consideration rather than condemnation. It's easy to make the other person wrong, but when it's someone you love, you're actually chipping away at the foundation of your relationship.

N—Never be mean to your mate. If couples would refrain from doing damage to each other's self-worth, there would be a major drop in the divorce rate. I would like nothing better than to be put out of business as a marriage counselor because there are too many happy couples.

E—Entice your partner to be romantic. Set the mood as early in the day as possible. If you want to have a romantic evening, it's best to begin before you get out of bed in the morning.

S—Sympathize with your mate. Your sympathy shows your willingness to connect with your mate in a way that he or she can find nowhere else in the world.

S—Safety allows partners to feel comfortable being tender with each other. Many people are afraid that their offerings of compassion will be thrown back in their faces, a fear that makes it seem safer to withhold tender actions. Make your partner feel safe in your love.

The song "Love Me Tender" didn't become a classic just because Elvis sang it. We all want to feel tenderness. If you've avoided this level of intimacy or withheld it, it's time to reconsider your actions. Life is so short. Let yourself give and feel at a level that will make you glad you're alive.

PART
8

Intimate

Love

The Importance of Romance

*W*ith all the distractions we have in our busy lives, it seems many couples never find the time to be romantic, and that can lead to love's demise. Romance needs to be a constant in your universe. Being romantic is not much work, and savoring romantic moments will actually strengthen your bond as a couple.

Romance is about getting closer. While there is a big difference between sex and romance, in most relationships, if you want the former to be great, you have to fully engage in the latter.

Most people don't try romantic activities because they simply don't know how. Here's a hint: there are no secrets to romance. Most of the time, everything we need to know is right under our noses. Anyone who has ever watched a romantic movie knows enough to get the ball rolling.

Through a little trial and error and lots of conversation, the two of you can create the kind of romance that would put Romeo and Juliet to shame. In many cases, all it takes is some encouragement to take a risk and a little appreciation for your partner's efforts (even if they fall a little short). Romance, like life, is seldom perfect, but it can be fulfilling, no matter how it differs from what you've seen on the silver screen.

The key is to make romance a normal part of your daily lives, and though it's not possible to live life like a Victorian novel, you can have a pretty hot twenty-first-century relationship. One of the tricks is to take advantage of any opportunity to learn more about romance and, most important, what it is that your partner perceives as romantic.

If you want to do more research on the subject, there are some wonderful books on romance, like Laura Corn's *101 Nights of Grrreat Romance*, which has separate sections for his eyes only and for her eyes only. There's also *1001 Ways to Be Romantic* by Gregory Godek, which has lots of little things you can do to make your partner feel wonderful and be inspired to return the favor.

What works for you may or may not work for the one you love. Remember, it's a gift of trust when your partner takes the risk of revealing his or her preferences to you. You may be surprised at how easy it is to create more sizzle and less static with a simple gesture or action.

Real-life romance is something I encourage you to engage in every day. Just give it a try. Many times it's all about the little things and just going with your heart. Trust that your desire to create romance is enough to get things started, and give it your own spin. The results will have you making your friends jealous.

Here are some tips to make your relationship truly romantic.

♡ *Have a loving conversation with your mate about what it is that turns him or her on. This is really the best way to make your relationship romantically enduring.*

♡ *Ask your partner to share a romantic fantasy with you, and share yours. Then try to avoid making love—dare ya!*

♡ *Make a grand gesture to show your love. Doing the extraordinary as a couple will stoke the fires and inspire a new level of depth. It also has the benefit of creating wonderful memories. So, arrange for the two of you to go on that hot-air balloon ride, or surprise your partner with tickets for a trip to some exotic land, or plan for that special night of passion, which can happen right at home or at a hotel. They all count, but sometimes just bringing home dinner from your favorite restaurant because you know your partner is too tired to cook or go out is the grandest of all gestures.*

♡ *Feeling deep within your core that you're with the right person is a total turn-on. There's nothing else like it on earth. Hold your partner in a loving embrace, and do it often. This is what real intimacy is all about.*

Make Him Your Hero

Virtually every guy wants the same thing from a woman—to be her hero. Think what you will, but for many men being the hero for their mate is more important than sex. Cynics might say it's because he thinks he might get a little, if his hero-ing is good enough, but I believe there are deeper reasons here.

When a woman looks adoringly into the eyes of a man and makes him feel like a dragon slayer, some knight-of-the-round-table gene is triggered and it makes a guy feel like a king. Unfortunately, the opportunities to be a hero, unless you're a soldier, a police officer, or a fireman, are somewhat limited. For us everyday guys, men need women to notice the hidden hero that resides in the hearts of us all.

I hate to give away a trade secret, but whenever a guy gets recognized for any quasi-heroic acts, like lending his cell phone and AAA card to your children so they can get home safely or finding a great deal on a new barbecue grill, it just makes his day. I can't tell you how amazing that little bit of recognition makes a guy feel. It's like everything he's ever done has been worth the effort.

I think this is one of those things that's hardwired into our brain circuitry. Perhaps our forefathers handed it down as they robbed from the rich and gave to the poor, or maybe it was from watching all those Errol Flynn movies. Whatever the reason, the way to a man's heart is to tell him he's your hero when he does something wonderful. It's also helpful to look at him the way you did when you first fell in love.

If you're good at holding a grudge, this process may be a bit hard for you, so let me give you a little motivation. By making your man feel like a hero, he will then become confident to perform increasingly heroic tasks. He may rescue you from an evil sorcerer on the back of his noble steed or take you on a romantic weekend getaway just because he feels like doing something gallant.

Making a man feel good about himself is not just a lady-like gesture; it is a way of inspiring the person you love to reach for the stars and perhaps pull one down for you. It also will help to keep the spark in your relationship alive because men express themselves romantically when they see that their partner respects and admires them.

Even if picking up the kids from soccer and grabbing a bucket of chicken after a tough joust at the office may not seem all that heroic (because you do it every day), let him know he's your white knight. I promise you it will be worth a chest of gold to him, and he'll be much more likely to take on the quest again. This way you might actually get the fairy tale.

Here are some tips to make your partner feel like a hero.

♡ *Say the words "You're my hero" or "Honey, you're amazing." Try a tiny attitude shift, so you can better see his heroic acts and let him know when you do.*

♡ *Get him an engraved gift (a picture frame, a watch, even a key chain) that tells him he's great at being your partner. Recognition is the strongest motivating force you can give.*

♡ *Dedicate a song to him on the local radio station, and set it up so he's listening. It could lead to a wonderful make-out session on the couch.*

Three Little Things for Her

*J*ust as you need to exercise and eat right to keep your body in shape, creating a conscious connection with the woman you love will keep your relationship emotionally fit. Many guys can get emotionally disconnected without realizing it. If you feel that you want to be closer to the woman you share your bed with, you need to find your way back—not just for the sake of your relationship but also for your own sense of well-being.

Sometimes self-absorption creates a barrier that prevents us from acting on the little signals that tell us it's time to connect with the woman we adore. Ignoring these signals indicates that you are too preoccupied with something other than your relationship. It can be work, money, or just the stress of life. If this is the case, try putting the rest of your life on hold for a moment, and reach out to her. When your relationship is working, it actually makes the rest of your life better.

Occasionally, subconscious anger can create behaviors that cause a man to take a step back. If you back up too far, you can fall off a cliff and into a chasm of pain and distrust that can cause irreparable damage.

Correcting this problem is much simpler than it may seem and doesn't require therapy or even reading a self-help book. Calling, complimenting, and sending a card to your sweetheart are three little things that will go far in making your connection deeper. Try it. I promise you'll enjoy the results.

Here's all you need to know about the three Cs: calling, compliments, and cards.

♡ *Call your lover at various times during the day. This will go a long way to increasing your connection with her. Try to phone when you're on the way to work, when you get a break of longer than five minutes, and when you're on your way home. Touching base throughout the day keeps your hearts and heads connected and reminds her that she's not all alone out there.*

♡ *Compliment your partner often. Knowing that you think highly of her and recognize the work she's doing on herself and for your relationship, as well as what she has contributed to your family and community, can make her day. Hearing you say "Wow!" when she comes down the stairs dressed up for an evening out will make her look even more radiant. Acknowledgements like that help keep you connected by letting her know she's desirable. We all need to feel that the one we have given our heart to also admires us.*

♡ *Send or give your partner a loving card. This is a tangible token that says you care. It takes a little time and trouble to pick out an appropriate card and to write something meaningful. That extra energy you put out will be well received. It will make your partner feel that you are willing to go the extra mile to make her feel loved. It will also make you feel better, because your partner's affectionate response will return the love you send in the card.*

The Chemistry of Love

*M*any people mistakenly think that sex is the most powerful force pulling us into relationships. Romantic love, a biological urge distinct from sexual arousal, is actually more powerful. The desire for romantic love can be more powerful than the will to live and much stronger than your sex drive.

Love produces some of the most powerful drugs on earth, and it all happens in our own brains and without ever taking a pill. So when we talk about the important role that chemistry plays in picking a partner, we're actually on the mark.

In *Why We Love*, Rutgers University anthropologist Helen Fisher (2004) writes about the distinct neural mechanisms of romantic love, which differs greatly from sexual attraction. Brain-scan studies show that romantic love activates places in the brain with a high concentration of receptors for dopamine, a chemical tied to motivation, euphoria, and addiction.

Yes, this chemical is the same one that gets triggered by certain stimulant drugs. So when you go through a breakup and the supply of chemicals is cut off, you actually go through a type of withdrawal, and this is why it can be so hard to let go of someone you've loved.

When we do find someone we click with, we want to believe it will last forever, and for a lucky few it will. Unfortunately, science tells us that for the vast majority of couples, this feeling will only last from one to three years. After that time, we (hopefully) begin to appreciate our commonality, rely on communication, and relax in the compassion of our relationships.

Additional studies by the University of San Francisco and professor Rebecca Turner show that another brain chemical, oxytocin, also gets released, but this usually happens after couples have been together for a while (Turner et al. 1999). A rise in the level of oxytocin comes from being touched. It makes us want to be physically close, and not just sexually. It heightens the feeling of bonding and can increase intimacy and receptiveness.

The research also shows that oxytocin appears at higher levels in women who are involved in committed relationships. The presence of this chemical also helps us to understand why men tend to feel more intimate after sex, for that's when their oxytocin reaches its peak.

These chemically based changes won't diminish your capacity for love. Think of them more as additions to what you already have. Feeling completely connected and cared for is really what intimate relationships are all about.

Even though your sexual desire may decrease in intensity, your natural need for a romantic connection will continue for many years to come.

Brain chemistry may get love started, but the real keys to lasting relationships are found in your heart and soul.

Here are some tips for using your natural brain chemistry to enhance your intimacy.

♡ *Bedtime cuddling helps sustain long-term intimate connections. If you or your partner needs space for sleeping, ask if you can snuggle before you shift to your own side of the bed. Those who engage in this activity also have more active sex lives.*

♡ *If you have a TV in the bedroom, get it out. Couples who have no TVs in the bedroom have more sex and greater intimacy. If you're a nighttime reader, put down your book and just be with your partner. You're going to cuddle more if there are no distractions, and that can only lead to a deeper connection. It doesn't mean you can never read or watch TV in bed. Just get out of it being a habit.*

Scavenger Hunt

$\mathcal{E}$very day I am on a mission to find something that will make my partner smile. Sometimes it's the easy fallback of taking her out to dinner; other evenings I'll light the fire and tell her an amusing story. On days when I have no time or energy, I might pick a flower from the yard and leave it on her nightstand.

The point is that it doesn't matter what I do or give. The idea is to bring a smile to her face, for when she's happy, I'm happy. In fact, the argument could be made that I do these things for myself because I reap the benefit.

Perhaps it's the cup of coffee that your mate brings you in the morning, so you can stay in bed a few minutes longer, or maybe the love of your life senses when you've had a long day and makes dinner for you. Some people come home with a bouquet of flowers, and others bring things they know their partners want or need. It usually doesn't take much to make someone feel loved.

Your partner will truly appreciate your taking the time to make his or her day a little bit more special. Taking this time can breathe new life into a tired relationship.

Remember, it's the thought that counts, and in this case, small and cheap, or even free, is just fine. You don't have to sell the farm to make your point. Showing that you care shouldn't cost you. If you do these small things well, it will make the big and difficult things much easier to deal with.

If these small gestures are something you'd like more of in your relationship, let your partner know. Don't expect your mate to read your mind. If you're unsure of how to start the process, just hand him or her this chapter. You can make up the rules as you go along.

Knowing that the light of your life is thinking of you when he or she is running errands, dealing with the kids, or trying to keep the boss happy can make you feel really loved. That emotion is what makes us get up in the morning to do it all over again.

If you don't have a desire to do little things to make your partner smile, there may be some resentment that I'd encourage you to take a look at. This isn't meant to be a burden. It's just one of those little things that keeps the heart fires burning.

Here are some tips for a successful scavenger hunt.

♡ *Suggest to your partner that you take turns spending a week doing one little thing a day for each other. Then talk about what it was like for both of you. Consider making it a regular thing.*

♡ Find that little thing your partner lost or couldn't locate any-where and bring it to her or him.

♡ Do the manly-man thing or the girly-girl thing. Many men say I love you by washing their mate's car and filling it with gas. To reciprocate, taking your man to a game, concert, or movie that he really wants to see is a great way to show your love.

Intimate Sex

One of the things that successful relationships all seem to have in common is that the couples in them share physical intimacy on a regular basis. Those who do this have the best chance of getting over the rough patches and maintaining a long-term relationship, because they seldom doubt the love of their partner.

After several years of being together, many couples may feel that their sex life has gotten comfortable, perhaps a little too comfortable. Couples in the prime of their lives often complain that they have sex less often than when they were single. Yet experts agree that although the "in love" feeling will fade in the near term, sex can get better and better with the passing of time and the deepening of intimacy.

If you want your sex life hotter and more intimate, getting what you want all starts by letting your partner know what you want. You could begin by asking him or her to read this chapter. Take time for what's most important: being together.

Remember that intimacy is built on a bedrock of trust, so always be conscious of your partner's comfort level.

There are dozens of ways to liven up your sex life and increase intimacy. You really just have to decide on something you think will work, and try it. What this process and others like it can help couples do is to build comfort and learn more about each other, which is what makes a person feel safe enough to be sexually open. The stability of a long-term relationship helps to create a healthy sex life because it's difficult to freeze out a person you are intimately and sexually attached to.

Couples who look for new ways of relating sexually and developing a deeper intimate connection may share other benefits. Besides a healthier relationship, they may enjoy better emotional and physical health. It's common knowledge that married people outlive their single counterparts. Mature couples also report that, though sex is less frequent than it was in years past, it is still fun, often more satisfying, and it enhances their ability to enjoy life.

So with all these reasons to work on and maintain an intimate relationship, the only question left is why you are still reading this book.

Here are some techniques that you can use in and out of bed to strengthen your intimacy with your partner.

♡ *Sex is obviously a large portion of intimacy, but it is only one part. Kissing or holding one another is also very important in the intimacy quotient. Share a ten-second hug and kiss when* you see each other at the end of the day. Who knows where it may lead?

♡ In order for a relationship to be truly intimate, affection has to be exchanged throughout the day. Encourage your partner to have coffee with you in the morning and to keep in touch during the day. Call your partner during breaks at work and on your way home. You can also e-mail. If you're the first one home, greet your partner at the door. These actions all help build intimacy and enhance your love life.

♡ Encourage your partner to put aside the bills, housework, and phone calls once in a while. Try making out on the sofa before going to bed, and experiment with having sex in different places or in different ways.

Ten Tips for Being More Thoughtful

*W*hen we first get together with our mates, we tend to put a lot of thought into our relationship. Over time, that way of being can get lost in the tornado of daily living. Here are ten tools to put the thoughtfulness back where it belongs.

1—Take time. Couples who connect daily, have date nights, and regularly take mini-vacations have more satisfying relationships. If both of you make your relationship your priority, it won't be hard to find the time to be together. Time is our most valuable commodity; share it with the one you love.

H—Hold hands. We don't touch enough; in fact, the average American couple only touches twice a day (Mehrabian 1971). If you don't share some nonsexual physical affection on a daily basis, you are touch-starving one another. Tactile deprivation leads to resentment.

O—Offer optimism. You don't have to be a Pollyanna to see the glass half full. If your partner is feeling low, give him or her a lift. Relationships require us to prepare for the worst while expecting the best and to be there for the ones we love.

U—Use understanding. "Seek rather to understand than to be understood" (from the Prayer of St. Francis) are some of the wisest words ever spoken. When your partner feels understood, he or she can love you more deeply and give you more of what you need.

G—Give gentleness. I believe in honesty, but I think that so-called brutal honesty is just an excuse to criticize someone. Get real with yourself and look at how much it hurts when someone you care about talks down to you in the name of "setting you straight." If you can't say it gently, don't say it until you can.

H—Help heal. When the one you cherish is going through a rough patch, extend yourself as much as possible. After a few years, we can become complacent about our partner's emotional ups and downs. If you offer your emotional support, it will make both of your lives more pleasant.

T—Think tenderly. Most of our energy is spent just trying to make it from one day to the next. By making tender gestures toward your mate, you end up making his or her life a bit sweeter. It's all about the little things.

F—Find forgiveness. If you are holding on to anger, it's time to give it up. Forgiveness is a necessity for a long-lasting relationship, and the sooner you find it, the better you will feel. Once forgiveness is earned, you need to put the transgression behind you.

U—Unite unselfishly. Share everything you can. Good relationships have very little to do with "me and mine." They are much more about "yours and ours."

L—Love limitlessly. When you love with your whole heart, your partner will feel it. It's an amazing sensation, and once you get it into your system, you will never want it to go away.

Being thoughtful costs you nothing, but it can give you one of the most valuable things in life: a wonderful relationship.

References

Fisher, H. 2004. *Why We Love: The Nature and Chemistry of Romantic Love.* New York: Henry Holt and Company.

Mehrabian, A. 1971. *Silent Messages.* Belmont, CA: Wadsworth.

National Sleep Foundation. 2008. 2008 Sleep in America Poll: Summary of Findings. Accessed March 2008.

Rich, J. 2003. *The Couple's Guide to Love and Money.* Oakland, CA: New Harbinger.

Turner, R., M. Altemus, T. Enos, B. Cooper, and T. McGuinness. 1999. Preliminary research on plasma oxytocin in normal cycling women: Investigating emotion and interpersonal distress. *Psychiatry* 62 (2): 97–113.

Barton Goldsmith, Ph.D., has more than twenty years of experience as a therapist and has been named one of the country's top relationship experts by *Cosmopolitan* magazine. His weekly newspaper column, *Emotional Fitness,* appears in more than two hundred newspapers. He also hosts a weekly radio show on KCLU/NPR, broadcast in the Los Angeles, Ventura, and Santa Barbara areas. Goldsmith is author of Emotional Fitness for Couples and has appeared on *CNN, Good Morning America, Fox & Friends, CBS News, NBC News, Beauty and the Geek,* and *The Greg Behrendt Show.* He regularly offers workshops to the public. More information is available online at www.bartongoldsmith.com.

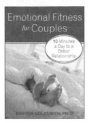